T0131634

THE
Human
TRINITY

Your Spirit Energy in Action

J. L. REYNOLDS

BALBOA.
PRESS

A DIVISION OF HAY HOUSE

Balboa Press books may be ordered through booksellers or by contacting:

Balboa Press
A Division of Hay House
1663 Liberty Drive
Bloomington, IN 47403
www.balboapress.com
1 (877) 407-4847

Because of the dynamic nature of the Internet, any web addresses or links contained in this book may have changed since publication and may no longer be valid. The views expressed in this work are solely those of the author and do not necessarily reflect the views of the publisher, and the publisher hereby disclaims any responsibility for them.

The author of this book does not dispense medical advice or prescribe the use of any technique as a form of treatment for physical, emotional, or medical problems without the advice of a physician, either directly or indirectly. The intent of the author is only to offer information of a general nature to help you in your quest for emotional and spiritual well-being. In the event you use any of the information in this book for yourself, which is your constitutional right, the author and the publisher assume no responsibility for your actions.

Any people depicted in stock imagery provided by Thinkstock are models, and such images are being used for illustrative purposes only.
Certain stock imagery © Thinkstock.

Print information available on the last page.

Library of Congress Control Number: 2015915793

ISBN: 978-1-5043-4137-0 (sc)
ISBN: 978-1-5043-4139-4 (hc)
ISBN: 978-1-5043-4138-7 (e)

Balboa Press rev. date: 11/16/2015

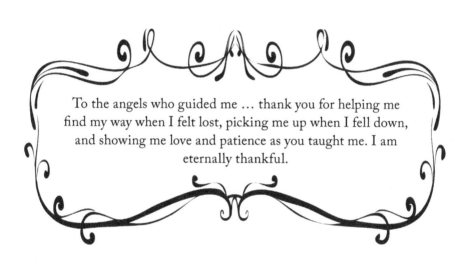

To the angels who guided me … thank you for helping me find my way when I felt lost, picking me up when I fell down, and showing me love and patience as you taught me. I am eternally thankful.

Contents

Preface

Have you ever wondered why it feels as though some people come at you like a fire but others seem so laid back that you suspect it would take a major crisis to crack their façade? The ability to show emotions or engage energetically with others is a gift of your spirit body. How you may initially react to situations also has ties to your spirit body type. At the moment life breathes into your form, your soul infuses your spirit body with the essence of your being, permeating your entire physical self with the essence of who you are, including the lessons learned in prior lifetimes. Our spirit body is a vital component of our being through which we experience life from an energetic perspective and receive information from our physical being. Together, these experiences contribute to our soul's growth over our lifetime. Through our spirit bodies, we connect to others, to the energetic aspect of our world, and to the divine. This connection to both the physical and ethereal worlds allows you to experience life with a fullness that would not have been possible otherwise.

As pure energy, your spirit body animates your human form while drawing in life-sustaining energy from the divine. Together, your physical body, soul, and spirit body form your human trinity. You are able to enact power over your human form while making decisions and living through experiences in your quest to achieve your soul's mission during this lifetime. Your spirit body also has the ability to release energy into your environment or direct it at others. In every moment of your life, your spirit body and physical body communicate with each other, giving your human existence a multidimensional life experience. It offers you the choice of experiencing life in the full range of human emotions, or not. This ability to express yourself energetically or through your physical body allows you to be "present" in your life and gives you the opportunity to experience life in all aspects—physical, spiritual, and emotional.

Your spirit body's shared communication network with your physical body allows them to share how they are feeling, whether they are injured, and if they need help or divine assistance. Through your human trinity, you access multiple versions of consciousness originating from your soul, spirit body, and physical body. This ability allows you to analyze your life experiences and situations from several perspectives simultaneously to determine the path you want to take. By using the gifts of your human trinity, you can enact change within your life and pull in positive energy from the divine, even though you may be experiencing a difficult or stressful life challenge.

As a conduit of divine energy, your spirit body infuses your entire human trinity with life-sustaining energy. It breathes in energy from your world and the divine, nourishing it and healing it when life experiences have hurt you or caused you pain. As with your physical body, there are times when you need to detoxify your spirit body to release the residual energy baggage that is holding you back. Sometimes, this residual energy was stuck in your soul and was brought with you when you incarnated in this lifetime. As a divine gift from the universe, your spirit body possesses characteristics that can be both a blessing and a challenge, depending on the situation. To be successful in managing your energy, it is important to understand how your spirit body directly affects your physical being and how you interpret life experiences through the filter of your spirit body.

Your spirit body allows you to connect with other human trinities through ethereal umbilical cord connections. Collectively, these cord connections form our human relationship matrix. This series of connections to other human trinities can support us when we are living through difficult life experiences, or when our faith wanes due to negative events that are beating us down. However, to benefit from the power of our matrix, we need to allow those to whom we connect help us when we need it, by accepting the positive energy they share. If we do not let their positive, supportive energy enter our spirit body, we can be limiting our ability to bounce back from difficult experiences and regain energetic balance in our lives. Sometimes, without the tethering support from our connections, our spirit body energy spins deeper and lower, increasing our sense of isolation or hopelessness. At times, we can all fall into a mind-set in which we forget that although we are in a very difficult life phase, it will not last forever, even though at the time it may feel that way. Sometimes, our connections become the safety net that catches us, or the rope we hold onto when it feels like the bottom drops out of our world.

In your life, you will have experiences that challenge, amaze, or thwart you on your soul's quest to learn and grow. As an energy being in the form of a human trinity, you have been gifted with the right to enact free will in your life. Regardless of what is happening in your life—good or bad—you have the ability to draw in energy from the universe or your physical environment to help you get back on your feet and try again. Each day, you have a choice of how you are going to use the free universal energy available to you and the gifts of your spirit body. Whether you use them for the greater good, to better yourselves energetically, or use them in ways that others feel are harmful, is ultimately your choice to make. Regardless of how you use this energy, it is always best to start by being your authentic self and aligning your actions with your true intent.

You have the ability to manifest good or bad things in your life. However, there are times that the bad things you are wishing on others boomerang and manifest in your own life. Each moment of your life, you have the divine gift to live out your free will in your daily life as long as you do not impinge on the free will or safety of another person. Whenever you use your energy to harm another, there are karmic impacts for doing so that may manifest in your life or in the lives of those you love. Taking back power over your energy and regaining control on how you use it is the first step in the process of personal healing and spiritual growth. This growth is essential to your life's journey to become the best version of yourself. The greatest gift you can give yourself is to practice using your energy to promote a heathy spirit body and manifest good in your life.

Chapter 1

YOUR HUMAN TRINITY

You are from the divine. As a human trinity, you are a finely tuned instrument with a degree of sensitivity to energy from people, from your physical environment, and from the universe. Your human form is composed of your soul, spirit body, and physical body. These three distinct parts of your energy-being integrate through your *sona*, which is the energy chakra that houses your soul throughout your physical lifetime. I call this three-in-one a *human trinity*. This idea is not as far-fetched as it may initially seem.

The life source of your human trinity is your soul. Your soul begins as a divine spark of energy that traverses time and space before entering your human form, causing your heart to beat for the first time. The moment your sona holds your soul and joins it to your physical and spirit bodies is the moment when your human trinity comes to life. However, many more months of growth and development are needed before it has the ability to survive outside the womb. When you are born, your physical and spirit bodies create the individual that is you. However, your growth does not stop when you are an infant. As you grow and develop, so do both your physical and spirit bodies until you have grown into the person you are as an adult. Then, your life experiences will continue to morph and change you as you learn lessons and experience life. Through your human trinity, you have been given the divine ability to process the events and make decisions about what you will do in your tomorrows.

ANCIENT KNOWLEDGE

Although in modern times people do not typically think of themselves as human trinities, it is not really a new concept. References to this concept can be found in ancient texts and scriptures. The fact that we are human trinities—having a soul, spirit body, and physical body—is part of a collection of ancient wisdom that has been around since the beginning of time. Some cultures have passed down this divine knowledge, while in others the knowledge has died with the elders of the tribes or civilizations. A vague reference to this phenomenon of human trinities is found in the Bible. Specifically, in Genesis chapter 1 verse 27, we are told how the universe created our being in the image of the divine one, which is a three-in-one.

In some cultures, they believed that they needed to preserve the physical body to allow for reanimation of the form sometime in the future. In essence, they believed that once the physical body reanimated, the person would rise from the dead, so to speak, and use the physical body. To preserve the body for this future animation, they would mummify their leaders and rulers. The idea that the body is just an animated vessel is not a new concept at all when you consider ancient wisdom. We even find references to the resurrection of the body in various religious teachings today. However, in other cultures, they believed that "resurrection" occurred, but not in the physical sense. Rather, it occurred when a soul reincarnated and inhabited different physical bodies in different lifetimes. Even today, various religions continue to agree that there is more to humanity than just the physical body and that there is an essence animating the physical body. They usually refer to this essence as our "soul" or "spirit."

When considering the human trinity and its gifts, it is important to consider each aspect of the human trinity in more detail. The most obvious aspect of our human trinity is our physical body. When we look around us, we see people at varying different stages of their lives. Some are young, and others are not. Regardless of their chronological age, they interact with the physical world through their physical bodies. Our physical bodies are the primary way we communicate with other physical beings, using both verbal and nonverbal communication. Through the different forms of communication, we have the ability to act upon our world in some way. Through your physical body, you act, think, and live while acting out your free will as you respond to the differing experiences that cross your life path. It is the animated "machine" of our human trinity.

All bodies have similar parts. In some respects, our physical being (a divinely made machine) has similarities to a car (a man-made machine). Cars have wheels to move around, a body, an electrical system, an engine, and they need some type of fuel to move about. In our physical state, we have a body, an engine (a heart energized by the sona), and an electrical system (our nervous system), and it too requires fuel (food, water, and air) to provide the energy needed to move around. Depending on who manufactures the car, there are differences in appearance. Our physical bodies are the same. Depending on the genetic code from our parents (the manufacturers), our physical bodies differ in a variety of physical attributes.

Unfortunately, the physical body is the part that might arouse tremendous self-hate at if it does not align with the cultural or another's definition of what the "preferred" attributes are for a body. There are many different reasons why people may hate their bodies. At times, people can be very hard on their physical bodies, and try to force their bodies to conform to an external definition of what is beautiful. What we may not consider is that we picked our physical body before birth. Before being too hard on it, or hating it too much, you may want to consider what benefits it offers, to try to see why you picked it to live out your human existence in this lifetime. The reality is, if your soul really did not want the body it was in, it would have rejected it before birth—causing a spontaneous abortion or stillbirth. Although the souls who do this may break their parents' hearts and throw them into despair, they are exercising their own free will. If you have experienced this type of loss, try to remind yourself that your child made a decision. Usually, this expulsion of the soul from the human trinity had nothing to do with whether you did anything wrong. Sometimes, by aborting the body early, the soul has decided to wait and come back in a body that it feels will be a better vessel to help it achieve its soul's journey. Some wait a short time, and others wait for decades to return to a human-trinity form. It is the soul's decision as to how quickly it will try again. For souls, their speed of return is sometimes dependent on whether their parents can release their souls enough to allow them to jump back into a new human trinity form. Unfortunately, the tighter you hold onto the soul of someone who has passed, the longer it takes for him or her to reincarnate.

However, considering you are reading this book—and did not abort your body prior to birth—then there is a reason why your soul accepted the body formed in utero. So, if you are not happy with it, have you considered whether the challenges of your physical body are part of your soul's mission? The physical body is your vessel. Within it, we all have benefits, weaknesses, strengths, and challenges to overcome. Consider what the potential benefits are within your human form. What does it allow you to do or achieve, or what protective role does it have that might not have been possible if you were in a different body? Embrace the aspects of your physical body that are benefiting you. For those you do not like, the first step of being happy is to accept what you cannot change about it and work on what you can change. Even though you do not consider it as perfect, it really is perfect for your soul's mission.

When we are overly critical of ourselves, it can affect the energy in the entire human trinity. It literally beats your spirit body, leaving it to bleed energy out into the cosmos over something it has no power to change. The more you beat yourself up with your words, thoughts, or actions, the ramifications of these injuries permeate your spirit body. When your physical body senses the dropping energy, it attempts to fill it up. The problem is that your physical body will rely on physical things to try to fill up your spirit body. This effort sometimes translates into falling into a pattern in which you are trying to increase the energy in your spirit body through food, spending money, hoarding, or other activities that make you feel "full" for short periods of time. Unfortunately, the only way to fill up your spirit body with energy is by closing the wounds in your spirit body, and drawing in energy from the universal energy grid to replenish what you lost. Trying to fill the energetic loss in another way simply does not work.

Your physical body is the machine, while your spirit body is the operator that puts your soul's essence into action. One of the primary roles of your spirit body is to animate the physical body. Through it, we process life events and experiences through all shades of energy. It also has an early warning system that senses the energy around you. When it senses danger to your human trinity, it sends an alarm to your brain to activate your flight-or-fight response. Just like our physical bodies, our spirit bodies have different body types. These are earth, air, fire, and water. I will talk more about these body types in another chapter. The important thing to be aware of is that we chose our differing spirit body types before we were born to help us as we navigate through life's journeys. Through our spirit body, we have the ability to connect to the ethereal plane.

Every day, you document how your life story affects your spirit body and records the essence of your experiences in your soul. At times, some of the pent-up residual energy can seep into your soul to be carried into your next lifetime. Your spirit body sustains your connection to the divine and the universal energy grid, as well as connecting you to others. When your physical body is quiet, it gives your spirit body the ability to reach to the Akashic records or into the ethereal plane. Through it, you receive divine inspiration, clarity, and guidance on difference courses of action.

Within our spirit body, we have energy centers through which we move energy. This energy system gives us the ability to test the energy of others. It also allows us to assess how differing decisions we make may affect those to whom we attach by sending pulses of energy out to our primary connections potentially affected by our decisions. How it resonates back serves as an indicator of how they will most likely react or how it can negatively impact their human trinities. Nothing we do is in a vacuum. Any energy we release into the world or the cosmos is like dropping a stone in the middle of a large puddle of water. Regardless of the size or weight of the stone, a rippling effect is seen. The same happens whenever you make decisions and release energy to bring it into being; the energetic ripple effect travels through the cords of those affected by your decision. Depending on the strength of your conviction or how strongly others oppose your decision, the impact can be gentle as a mild ripple, to a tsunami wave of energy rushing through the cord and throwing the energy of another or yourself into a spin. Even if you do something with the best of intentions, how it is experienced by another may not be as positive as you had hoped.

Your spirit body provides the energy that animates your physical body. It superimposes on your physical body, it can act in tandem with it, or independently reach to the divine to draw energy into your human trinity. Through our spirit bodies and physical bodies, we experience the world around us from both a physical and an energetic perspective. Although our physical and spirit bodies are superimposed on each other, they have the ability to act both together or independently. This gives people the ability to distance themselves from highly emotional situations almost as though they were a bystander, watching the situation unfold. Our energetic form gives us the ability to interact with both the physical and ethereal worlds at the same time. Energetically, we can leverage our spirit body energy to help calm our physical body in times of stress or uncertainty.

Your spirit body is also in constant communication with your soul. Through your spirit body's interpretation of your life experiences, it documents within your soul the essence of what you learned. Together, they express the essence of you to the world. Even though your soul knows what major life lessons it is destined to experience, it does not share this with the spirit body. Sometimes, by knowing the life lessons decreed by fate, one may be tempted to try to end the life journey rather than attempt to overcome what he or she may perceive as a mountain of struggle. Even if you find the challenge daunting, your soul would never willingly pick up a journey that it did not think it had a reasonable chance of successfully completing and achieving growth from the experience.

Your soul is the divine spark of energy within you that is the essence of who you are. It is a source of powerful energy your sona drives through your spirit body to animate it. It also instills life into our human trinity. Without a soul, your heart cannot beat. Your central nervous system will shut down forever, and your physical and spirit bodies will decay and break down into energy forms that are recycled. The physical body returns to dust, and the spirit body returns as energy to the universal grid to be recycled. Even though the soul disconnects from the human trinity, there are times that the spirit body remains connected to the soul. This occurs only if the soul has not gone to the light. I will talk more about this phenomenon later in the book.

Your soul infuses your spirit body with the essence and resonance of who you are, what you will do, and what you will not do. It communicates directly with your spirit body to share what is to your soul's highest good. Through it, your internal voice warns you if you are doing things that are not in its best interest. This is the part of you that plays the role of your conscience and reminds you of what the "right" thing is, regardless of whether you do it. Your soul is the quiet voice within you giving you guidance on how to approach situations. Although it is imperfect, it remembers the major mistakes from prior lives and tries to guide you away from repeating actions that will limit it in its growth. It also reminds you that if you continue acting in a specific way, you cannot expect the outcome to change. It also is where your spirit body records what you learn in this lifetime as it continues its quest to grow and to reach toward divinity of being … to be as the angels. In essence, your soul is the navigation system of your human trinity. It provides you with a map of your life and sends this information to your spirit body to help your human trinity navigate through life.

In comparing the concept of the human trinity to ancient wisdom, the greater soul is the divine spark of energy that infuses your person with the essence of who you are. This "soul" referenced in holy books is what is punished due to "sins" in the current lifetime. Within it, we carry the knowledge acquired through each lifetime. Some of you can easily resource this prior life knowledge using meditation or through your spirit body's ability to access the divine. It is an innate knowing of things, people, or events that you would have no other way of knowing unless you actually lived them. After the human trinity expires, this energy returns to the divine. At that time, it undergoes a "debrief" of your life's work, including answering the tough questions on why you did what you did to others or to yourself.

MULTIPLE CONSCIOUSNESS

Through our human trinity, we achieve consciousness in our lives. Typically, when we think of our consciousness, we think of how our minds process information. However, we actually have three levels of consciousness. For each aspect of our human trinity, we have a level of consciousness attributable to it. At any given time, we receive information from all three aspects of our human trinity, each viewing life and the events we experience from its perspective. The ability to process information in a multidimensional way allows us to grasp the ramifications of our actions within our daily lives. Our multiple consciousness, or presence of being, gives us the ability to be present in any of our life situations and to fully experience life in all shades of emotions if we choose to do so. This ability allows our human trinity to process situations through our physical body and spirit body, as well as through the lens of our soul.

Our consciousness through the physical body is what shares information with our human trinity regarding our physical environment. In this realm of consciousness, we interact with other physical beings on a human level and feel pain, happiness, and a host of other feelings. Through our physical bodies we communicate with others and share information, thoughts, and preferences within our lives. Your physical body also assesses events from the perspective of "What is in it for me?" or "How can I benefit in a tangible way?" This is not a bad thing at all. If we are not trying to achieve "wins" in our lives, and continually try to give everyone else what they need, our own physical needs may not be met. Over time, this may make us feel used or angry that we are constantly giving in to everyone else. From this view of our consciousness, we consider our physical responses, wants, and needs in respect to the potential outcome. However, you also have consciousness information shared with your brain that originates within your spirit body. When your spirit body processes information it receives from the energetic world around you, or energetic impacts of actions and events, it funnels this information to your brain stem, sharing it with your brain. Through your soul, you view the event in light of the best possible outcome that leads you farther on your path to become the best version of who you are.

We typically do not consider consciousness when we are asleep. However, through our sleep, we are still functioning within a frame of consciousness. During our physical body's sleep, our spirit body and soul are still active. This is when the noise in the physical body automatically quiets to allow the spirit body and soul to communicate with it without competition from our physical being. At this time, as our spirit body processes the day's events, it informs the brain on how it interpreted these events. In this state, your spirit body shares information that forces your brain to review the day's events and to file information away that is deemed important for future reference.

Even when you are awake, when your brain is processing information, you may not be aware that your spirit body is also processing the information and forms part of your consciousness. However, if something occurs that leaves the physical body unable to process information, your spirit body continues to assess the situation from a very detached, almost clinical perspective. The reason for this is that the brain isn't online to translate the information and invoke an emotional response to the stimuli. This is a very strange feeling when it occurs. It is as though you are on the outside looking down on the events that are occurring. At all times, your spirit body is aware of what is happening in your life, and it has feelings or reactions related to how the events affect it. Once communication is restored with the physical body, the brain triggers the emotional response that aligns with the spirit body's reaction. I will talk more about how this works in a later chapter.

Your soul also forms part of your consciousness. As you go through life, it assesses what you are doing, and it considers how you acted in other lifetimes in similar situations as well as the outcome from those prior experiences. It determines whether you are doing something "wrong" and notifies the brain stem through the spirit body to the physical body that it needs to try a different approach. Through your soul you have awareness at a subconscious level of the past lives and prior experiences. It is conscious of your authentic self and knows when the human trinity acts in ways that are outside of who you are. This process can generate angst within the human trinity. This is where your conscience comes into play. When you do something that your soul knows is wrong, it becomes the nagging voice in your head permeating your spirit body, letting you know that no matter how much your brain is trying to justify what you did, it was wrong, against the rules of the universe, or not in your soul's best interest.

Through our human trinities, we live out our human existence. We interact with others, we send out energy, and we communicate with both the physical and the ethereal realms. In our physical state, we share energy through physical touch and act out the decisions we make, thereby directing our life paths. Our human trinity gives us the ability to be in continual contact with our physical and spirit side while giving us a built-in compass that helps us make decisions that are to our highest good. Each moment of the day, we unconsciously and consciously decide how we are going to use our energy.

Whenever you release any energy into your world, you are solely responsible for the ramifications of its use. Unfortunately, when people do things to hurt others, they are creating a karmic debt in the universe, which will eventually repatriate and cause havoc in their lives. Sometimes, the debt returns much later in their lives, leaving them wondering why bad things are happening to them. However, there are times that bad things happen which are no fault of their own. It may the result of negative energy sent their way, or it may simply be part of their destiny. Whenever bad things are happening in your life, examine your actions to determine whether you did something in the past that is contributing to what is happening in your life. Unfortunately, if past actions are affecting your present, you may not be able to stop your energy from repatriating. However, you can try to mitigate the karmic outpouring by rectifying what you previously did.

Through our human trinity, we have the ability to draw in energy from our world to nourish our spirit body and release negative energy back to the universe that is weighing us down or blocking our soul's progress. It gives us the power of choice. People can choose to focus only on the physical aspects of their existence and to ignore all spiritual energy or help from the cosmos. If people do this, they are in essence telling the universe that they can do it themselves. Conversely, people can choose to live their lives focusing on the spiritual side of themselves.

Most of us are somewhere in the middle between physical and spiritual reliance in our lives. Regardless of the path you choose, it is your decision.

Our human trinity gives us the ability to send and receive energy from those around us. We can even choose to draw in healing energy from the universe to promote healing within our human trinity. The flexibility of choice it gives us is vast. During our lifetime, this ability to choose is ours until our human trinity's expiration date. The blessing is that regardless of which stance we take regarding our spirituality, we have the ability to change our minds whenever we please. The flexibility in how we use our human trinity to live out our human existence is critical to the success of our soul's life mission.

Your human trinity is a powerful entity through which you live in both the physical and ethereal worlds simultaneously. The fact that we are human trinities allows us to have the opportunity to debate with ourselves on the best course of action in any situation. So, why was it so important that we are a three-in-one? It is all about our divine right of free choice. We have the choice to do the "right" thing or what some may think is the "wrong" thing regardless of what our soul indicates we should do. You are probably wondering how that can be. Is not the role of our spirit body to live out the divine essence of our soul? The answer is yes. However, we have physical desires that resonate back into our spirit body. A dilemma may start as our spirit body struggles to reconcile what is "best" for our human trinity. We have the free will to live out our lives in the manner that we choose. Problems arise because our spirit body wants to satisfy our physical wants while achieving our soul's divine mandate in our lives. At times, the desires of each aspect of us are dramatically different. The ramifications of our actions can also be very different and lead us down a path that may not be in our soul's best interest.

Regardless of the path taken, having three "heads" to consider what action you will take is advantageous to our human trinity. However, it can help us only if we consider all of the information received from them before making a choice. These perspectives come from the energetic world, another from the physical, and the third from our soul. As a human trinity, at any time, our soul, spirit body, or physical body can fight for supremacy to manifest its desires. You may have heard the maxim "the devil made me do it," or you may have seen representations of someone with a devil on one shoulder and an angel on the other. Sometimes the "devil" is our own desires and wishes for instant gratification within our physical being, even if the result is not in our human trinity's best interest. The angel is our soul telling our spirit body to take a different path that is more selfless.

The angel is often your soul talking to you, telling you to step away from a temptation or from doing something that might feel good in the moment, but will leave you filled with regrets afterward. Your spirit body is stuck in the middle, trying to balance the highest good of your soul with your physical wants. However, your spirit body is not a bystander in this tug-of-war. It also contributes to the discussion and uses energy to assess the potential outcome of a decision. For some, it reaches to the ethereal plane to access the Akashic records to assess the results of the possible decisions. This process can create a three-way debate that the spirit body tries to resolve to achieve a win-win-win solution that mitigates harm or negative karma for the human trinity.

However, these three voices can create confusion when we are making decisions. At one time or another, we all find ourselves in a situation where we struggle to make a decision and determine what the right thing to do is compared to what we really want. By giving us a multidimensional human trinity, the divine entity of life has given us a great gift of choice. Unfortunately, there are times it is too much choice. The result is an internal debate, with your "best" side fighting with your "worst" side and your spirit body; none of them are willing to negotiate a deal to achieve the best possible outcome for all aspects of your human trinity. When people makes selfish decisions that benefit themselves but are "wrong" in some way, their needs and desires have overtaken their divine essence and they have done something that was not to their highest good. Regardless of the decisions we make, they will affect our lives in some way.

Within your human trinity, the physical body is often the loudest in expressing its physical wants and desires, followed by the spirit body; your soul's voice is the quietest of all. At times, it is a whisper in the raging battle for supremacy in our human trinity. Although we may not always listen to what our souls are trying to communicate, they always give us guidance. Our souls are imperfect, with challenges to overcome and strengths to build upon. Sometimes, it is simply making a decision of who you want to become and taking the necessary steps to reinvent yourself in that image. It is our job to help our souls learn from our life lessons to promote their growth and ability to achieve their highest good in our lives. Depending on a number of factors, some people may have more soul growth to achieve in this lifetime than others do. Remember, it is not a competition. Your journey is just that … yours. Each day, you have a new opportunity to try to make the most of it and help your soul achieve its highest good. However, we all can fall victim to shutting down the voices from our soul and spirit body in favor of a driving physical desire or need. Even though we hear our soul and spirit body telling our physical being what we should do, our human trinity honors the mandate to practice free will. Since our physical body is what we use to act on our life's mission, it has the ability to override what our soul or spirit body indicates we should do whenever it chooses to do so.

When we are receiving conflicting messages from the three aspects of our human trinity, it can be difficult to separate the information coming from the physical body, spirit body, and soul. However, by considering the type of information received, it can be a little easier to figure out which of your multiple consciousnesses is providing the information. In these internal debates, your brain tends to provide the historical facts that it has stored regarding similar situations. At times, it is unfailingly logical. It concludes that if "X" happened in the past, followed by "Y," then "Y" is *definitely* going to happen again, regardless of whether it is true in these specific circumstances. It is one of the ways that your physical body protects itself. When it knows that "X" generates some sort of negative outcome "Y," it will tell your trinity not to repeat history, that nothing good will come from it. However, your spirit body also is involved in this communication. If you previously went through a similar experience, your spirit body reminds your brain of how you felt the last time. This is where the residual energy associated with the event that is stuck in your spirit body rises to the surface. At times, it rushes back as overwhelming hurt or emotionally charged energy that rushes to your brain stem for processing by the physical body.

Sometimes, traumatic or hurtful residual energy can profoundly affect how your brain sees and interprets the information received in the current situation. Essentially, as your brain tries to process the information from the new event through the lens of the historical event's information supplied by the physical and spirit body, it skews the incoming data from the new situation that your brain perceives. In turn, your brain will see issues or red flags in the current situation. The problem is that these issues may not even be present in the current event, although there are similarities between an old experience and a current one. In addition, all the feelings your spirit body stuffed down as residual energy is reenergized and infuses your human trinity. This process can generate an overstimulated, over-the-top response to a situation in which there may not even be a real issue. Neither your physical body nor your spirit body wants to repeat a life experience that can become soul destroying. This is especially true if your human trinity was profoundly hurt the last time you were in a similar situation and your human trinity has struggled to overcome the past hurt.

The fight within the human trinity begins whenever your wants and desires are powerful, but your spirit body and soul are yelling that continuing down the path to that desire is going to derail or impede your soul's mission or growth in some way. Unfortunately, as hard as we try, sometimes we give in to our baser needs. If the desire is for a relationship with a person that is not in your highest good, if your physical body takes over and engages in a relationship with the person, you may end up hurt badly, leaving you to struggle to move past the trauma experienced with him or her. If the desire is for an object, you might end up spending a lot of money to acquire it, leaving you struggling for years to dig yourself out of a financial mess. When you desire personal recognition, you may end up with attention that you really did not want to receive.

When one makes decisions only to satisfy the physical being and the soul and spirit body do not believe they are to the highest good, this situation often leads to results the individual eventually regrets to some degree. Even if you do not regret the action immediately, karma may swoop in and let your trinity know that it made a small mistake, or at the other end of the spectrum, that it was a serious error in judgment. Regardless of any decision you make, through your human trinity you have the ability to assess a situation from several different perspectives. Every time you make a decision, you are taking another step in your life's journey. Sometimes the steps lead to something that is wonderful and fulfilling. Other times, it leads to regrets and the realization that there was a better way.

The most important gift of our human trinity is the ability to reassess our prior decisions, consider the ramifications, and learn from what we did well and from where we may have gone wrong. In life, we often learn the most from our biggest "mistakes." The reality is that we are more likely to revisit decisions or actions that had negative consequences or outcomes to determine the cause, than to reflect on what we have done well. A profound gift of our human trinity is our ability to analyze situations to see what we did wrong and generate ideas of what we can do differently in order to move forward, fix prior mistakes, or simply avoid making the same mistake in the future. This is where the gift of forgiveness is powerful. Sometimes, we most need to forgive ourselves.

Chapter 2

CHAKRA ENERGY IN YOUR SPIRIT BODY

There is a common misconception that chakra energy is within your physical body. In actuality, it is within your spirit body. The reason for this confusion is the effectiveness of your spirit body in aligning itself, superimposing itself, and integrating with your physical body. The two-way communication network between the two within your human trinity is so highly developed and efficient it can be difficult to determine where this energy originates. Each chakra is responsible for managing different aspects or types of energy, moving them through your spirit body, and helping your human trinity focus more or less energy on different aspects of yourself whenever it is needed. Through the differing focuses or pushing of energy from different chakras, your energy is stirred and you can be motivated to move, do something, or change something in your quest to pursue your human trinity's life goals.

Your chakras are just one element of your spirit body's energy transportation system. Each chakra has an important role in infusing your entire spirit body with energy, which radiates through your entire human trinity. It achieves this through the secondary energy transportation systems, including the meridians and the energetic structure of your spirit body. Depending on your spirit body type and your sona, how you drive energy through your chakras and into your spirit body differs. When your sona connects your human trinity into a single unit of humanity, it connects in a simple loop or infinity loop pattern. Although this is a simplified version of the multidimensional way your sona drives energy, when you flatten the movement, it represents the primary direction of energy flow.

If you have an infinity-loop sona, you may also have internal organs flipped in either the upper or the lower portion of your physical body. I suspect that the differing positions of the organs in the physical body are the reason why the infinity-loop sona forms. This is only one aspect of your energy driver. Another is your *polarity*. The easiest way to think of your polarity is to consider the direction of a clock. Those who have energy driven through their spirit body in a clockwise fashion have one polarity type, while those with energy going in a counterclockwise direction have a different polarity. For those with a simple loop pattern of energy movement, their energy moves either clockwise or counterclockwise through their spirit body. However, in those with an infinity-loop sona, energy movement is far more complex. For them, it is like having two smaller clocks within a single larger clock. In the clock at the top of their body, energy moves in either a clockwise or a counterclockwise direction. However, in the second clock, their energy is driven in the opposite direction. This creates a different polarity type for those affected by it.

There is no "best" direction of energy movement. Rather, the right direction is the one in which your energy is accustomed to flow. To move energy quickly, your sona drives energy through your chakras. You also have the ability to draw in energy through your chakras. For more information on how your sona connects your spirit body and physical body and drives energy throughout your human trinity, refer to my book *Taking Back Your Joy of Living.*

Your chakras are part of the primary transportation system of your spirit body that draws in universal energy needed to nourish your human trinity. If there is a blockage in energy within a chakra, it can affect your spirit's ability to move energy through this chakra. Energy that enters your spirit body from others with a cord connection to one of your chakras can also affect your energy movement. Whenever your energy is sluggish as it moves through a chakra, or too much energy passes out of your spirit body into a shared cord with another, it can leave you feeling sluggish. At times, when the energy loss or an influx of energy is significant, it can make you feel like your life is spinning out of control, that you are powerless, or that you are a prisoner within your own body. Whenever this happens, it can be challenging to determine which chakra is affected and whether it is the result of energy residue buildup within your spirit body or because you are sharing or receiving too much energy from another.

At times, your chakras do not move energy effectively due to an energy attack, in which another has struck out in anger, frustration, or any other negative emotion and their energy has struck a direct hit on the chakra. It might even be an indirect energy strike that occurs when you walk through an energy minefield and the latent energy residue strikes your spirit body and causes injury. This can happen if you enter a room where two people are engaged in some type of altercation. The moment you feel uncomfortable, prickly, or like your hair is standing up on your body, the energy has struck your spirit body. It is important to remember that whenever your spirit body is injured, it bleeds energy. Whenever this happens, there can be a sudden drop of energy, causing a loss of energetic control within you, which makes your spirit body feel unbalanced. The result is that your energy spins or churns within you. This effect might manifest as a headache, racing thoughts, whirling energy in your stomach, or a general sense of unease, to name a few.

Spinning or whirling energy can also be the result of external forces or decisions of others in a power position that interfere with your energy movement by forcing you to act in a way that is against your personal beliefs. This can occur simply when someone expects you to do something in one way but the same results are achieved if you follow your own approach. Even though it is a difference of opinion, if you feel forced to do something you do not want to do, your spirit body will react. The sense of unease magnifies if your human trinity feels it is forced to act in a way that is against its fundamental beliefs or personal code of ethics, or if you do something that you feel is somehow wrong. Whenever you consciously decide to move your physical body (brain) in a way that opposes your soul and spirit body, this causes an energetic rift within your human trinity.

However, the disruption of energy in your spirit body might be partly due to the ego overtaking the human trinity because it feels entitled or justified to act in a specific way. When this occurs, energy from other chakras within the spirit body floods the 'will' chakra, in essence starving the other energy centers. Unfortunately, anything that results in a loss of power within a chakra, or the overstimulation of energy within other chakras, allowing them to be predominant, cause a significant imbalance of energy within the human trinity. Whenever you physically do anything that is in opposition to what your spirit body and soul believe is "right," or there is an imbalance of energy flowing through the chakras, it can result in a powerful churning of energy within you that can lead to insomnia or even a panic disorder. If your spirit body and soul are not happy with your physical body's actions, or if chakras are unbalanced, this discomfort transfers into the physical body. Part of this angst or whirling energy is due to the soul sensing a loss of control within the human trinity or it is worrying that you may be failing a life lesson. Remember, it has a job to do in this lifetime.

The chakras within your spirit body possess differing types of energy that gain predominance at various times during your life. This is quite normal. If you are in a homeostatic state and your life is at complete peace, the energy moving through all the chakras and into your human trinity is relatively equal. However, for most of us, our different chakras amplify energy in differing strengths to help move our human trinity in different ways. Some of the stimulation of our chakras comes from our sona. At other times, it comes directly from our physical body. Essentially, our physical wants and/or needs can stimulate differing chakras as it tries to get the spirit body to draw in more energy to manifest its desires.

Regardless of whether you embrace the belief that there are seven or eight chakras, it is more important to consider the types of energy each possesses. Your sona is usually slightly below the heart chakra toward the side of your spirit body. It may align to either the left or the right of your spirit body. However, it is not in direct alignment with the other seven chakras. For those of you who are new to chakra energy, the first chakra is your base chakra. This one is on your median line through your body, and it is located at the bottom of your pelvis. The uppermost chakra is just above the top of your head. The main chakras, excluding the sona, are from one to seven, with the base being the first chakra and the crown chakra being the seventh. Your sona is your eighth chakra. Each chakra supports a specific type of energetic function with your spirit body. Image 1 illustrates the alignment of chakras in your spirit body and the essence of the energy type that moves through each chakra.

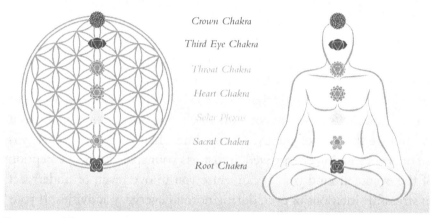

Image 1: Illustration of chakras and their corresponding energy types.

When in a steady state, chakras in your spirit body align with specific areas within your physical body. However, for those of you who are not grounded well, your spirit body's alignment might be offset to the left or right, or it might sit high or low as compared to your physical body. Whenever your spirit body does not superimpose in perfect alignment on your physical body, this positioning can cause chakra energy to be off and you may feel as though you are not yourself. Some may not feel comfortable within their physical body or may feel that they do not fit into their own skin. This can be short-term or can be a long-term result of not balancing your energy. It can also happen if your chakras are full of residual energy and cannot move energy through them efficiently. The energetic resonance of the chakras presents as different color waves that align with the function of the specific chakra.

Although each chakra has an energy type associated with it, they do not act alone. This dynamic energy system allows chakra-to-chakra exchange of information. At times, even though the energy enters the crown chakra or root chakra, a different chakra processes the energy. Energy can move through chakras in a variety of ways. It moves up, down, or out the sides into meridians or into the energetic fabric of your spirit body. It is similar to how blood moves within your body. From a highly simplified perspective, your blood is pushed out of the heart (sona) and goes though the main arteries (chakras), into the veins (meridians) and then into your capillaries (the energetic fabric of your spirit body). Although the sona is the driving force that sustains life within the human trinity form, you have the ability to draw in universal energy in a number of ways to nourish your spirit body.

Through this dynamic energy movement, your spirit body is able to nourish all aspects of itself to maintain its energetic health. The beauty of chakra energy is that even though it has a natural pattern of energy movement, you can consciously change its direction or act on it to improve the flow of energy. At any time when your chakra energy is off or is not moving energy well, it distorts your spirit body's perception of the events around you. It can cause you to overreact, or underreact in stressful situations or even during normal everyday activities. If your energy flow is slow, you might feel as though you are on the outside looking in on yourself or you might feel numb when you logically think you should be reacting. If it is moving too fast, you may feel like you are spinning.

Energy coming through energetic umbilical cord connections from others can profoundly affect energy movement through your chakras, since the cords connect directly to your main chakras. It is much more difficult for someone to establish a strong umbilical cord connection to a meridian or directly to an area on your spirit body that is not a chakra. Regardless of whether the energy is from within your spirit body or originates from others, your chakra energy is important to the continued health of your spirit body. When reviewing the chakra energies, it is important to consider the general purpose of the chakra within your spirit body, and what happens when it is blocked or when energy sludge within it is slowing down energy movement. This information can be very helpful when you are trying to realign your energy or resolve a disruption of energy movement within your spirit body which has a direct effect on your entire human trinity.

CROWN CHAKRA

Your crown chakra aligns with the top of the head on the physical body, and it is illustrated with purple-colored energy. The resonance of the color purple signifies divine protection and wisdom. The color of the energy within this chakra can vary from a very light lavender hue to a deep purple color that almost looks black. Depending on whether the person is accessing divine knowledge, the concentration of this energy also varies. When you are in communication with the divine, the energy is very pale and reaches far above your head. This is because your energy is intermingling with divine energy, causing it to appear more diffuse and lighter. In a steady state, the color is a light to medium purple in color and has a very small reach above the top of your head. This is the state where you are accessing energy around you but are not directly downloading information from divine records or knowledge. Most of us are in this steady state when we are *not* practicing yoga, prayer, or meditation, or when we are not actively trying to access divine knowledge and energy. These activities tend to modify our state of consciousness within our spirit bodies.

The strength of this chakra depends on how often you access universal knowledge or reach to the divine for knowledge, guidance, or spiritual enlightenment. For some people, this chakra energy is so effective in reaching the divine that they have the ability to understand and interpret ancient teachings or writings. Through this center, you gain the awareness that you are not alone … that there is something much bigger than you who helps you achieve your soul's goals in this lifetime. If you allow the energy to reach to the ethereal world, the divine shares insights and intuition, giving you guidance on how to resolve issues. Although you cannot "see" how the problem will be resolved, there is an innate knowing the situation will resolve in a way that is neutral, positive, or negative. If the outcome is going to be positive, this contributes to a feeling of peace infusing your spirit body.

This chakra also gives you the ability to send out energetic "feelers" to sense energy within your physical environment. This is how you will know whether negative energy directed at you is swirling in the cosmos. These feelers facilitate connections to the divine and the ethereal world. Divine inspiration transfers to your human trinity through this connection. Through this connection and the information you receive, you develop your own sense of what is true and valid spiritually within your life.

When reaching to the divine, this chakra allows you to partially disconnect from the physical body while connecting to the divine source of esoteric knowledge. Through this center, you can connect to the Akashic records of your prior lives and channel information from the divine. Some people are able to access ancient wisdom through this chakra and gain the knowledge needed to decipher ancient texts or puzzles. This is also the energy center used when you are testing the energetic resonance of another person against your own. Whenever someone tells your human trinity anything, when this chakra runs effectively, you can ping his or her energy to determine whether it resonates similarly to yours. If it doesn't, it sends a pulse back through the chakra letting you know that the information received does not resonate with your spirit body at that time. It does not necessarily mean that it is wrong, only that it does not resonate in the same way as you do.

Whenever there is damage to this center or the energy movement is stuck or not moving well, it affects your spiritual connection to the divine. It can affect your human trinity's ability to connect to the divine. Whenever you lose the ability to connect to the divine, this separation can generate the feeling that you are all alone in the world even though you may have many people around you. In addition, energetic interference with this chakra can skew your perception or affect your magnetism ... either of which makes you susceptible to negative attachments to this chakra. It makes it difficult to determine for yourself whether the information shared by others is what you would have believed had the chakra been functioning properly. When this chakra energy is sluggish, there is a long delay between the times you test the energy of another or of a thought and when you receive feedback on it, if you even receive any feedback from the energetic ping. This situation can leave you wondering whether it aligns with your resonance. Without this connection to the divine, the human trinity might seek out someone or a group of people who he or she believes have a strong connection to the ethereal world. It may leave you completely susceptible to blindly trusting the teachings of someone, never questioning whether it is in your human trinity's best interest to follow these teachings.

BROW/THIRD EYE CHAKRA

The next chakra is in the area of your spirit body that aligns with the center of your forehead. Some call this the brow chakra or third eye chakra. I personally use these terms interchangeably. From an energy perspective, the bottom of this chakra aligns with your eyebrows. The color resonance of this chakra is dark blue, signifying the processing of information from an analytical, detached manner rather than an emotional perspective. Depending on the person and the situation, the blue color can be as light as a gray blue or as dark as a blue-black hue.

The brow chakra is associated with the essence of awareness. This includes awareness of the physical, ethereal, energetic, and spiritual realms. This chakra enables you to channel and focus your thoughts when requesting help from the divine to manifest good in your life. Through this chakra, your spirit body has the ability to see what is ahead of you even though you cannot see it with your physical eyes. It is the energy center of perception where you attend to nuances in energy and physical micro-movements that reveal how others feel or are reacting even though they are trying to hide this from you.

Intuition is also attributable to this energy center. From this energy center, your spirit body can draw in information from your world, others, and the divine. As it processes this information, your spirit body generates an innate sense of knowing about something or someone when there is no physical way that you could know this information. Through this center, you process information received from the divine or from the energy sensed around you before forwarding the results of this energetic processing to the throat chakra. This is the eye visionaries see through and dream of what could be, not necessarily what is in existence today. Through this chakra, you can achieve clarity of thought.

During meditation, this is where divine inspiration is processed and revealed to your physical being. If you know someone who is a daydreamer, there is a good chance that this person has very strong or voluminous energy flowing through his or her brow chakra. This is also the center through which people "see" spirits or visual communications from spirits. Through this center, the souls of others can connect telepathically and send messages. For some gifted people, this is where they see messages from the spirit world in the form of visions, flashes of intuition, or movie clips as the spirit person is sharing information with them. Psychics use their crown chakra to access the Akashic records on your behalf and their third eye chakra to interpret the information received. Essentially, they are using their third eye to "read" the information if it is in the form of images or text. Those who are very skilled and practiced using their crown and third eye chakra energy can tell you things that have happened in your past or things that are destined to occur in your future, depending on the choices you make. This also means that they are interpreting what they see through the lens of their brow chakra.

Whenever people have blockages in their energy movement through this chakra, it is more challenging to manifest what they want or need. This situation is worse if you are also struggling to see what you are trying to manifest. If you cannot see it, it is much harder to focus your intent and draw the energy needed from the universal energy grid to manifest what you desire in the physical plane. Blocks or stagnation of energy within the third eye chakra fragments information your spirit body receives from the divine. The result is that the information received is disjointed, confusing, or missing critical components, making it hard to determine what the original communication was or to understand the direction you are given by the divine. The outcome is that your spirit body becomes confused or may feel that it has lost the ability to communicate with the divine or to think clearly. It also limits your ability to focus your thoughts, affecting the consciousness of the spirit body.

Whenever there is damage to this center or energy cannot move freely through it, your spirit body's ability to see is limited. Whenever this occurs, it limits the human trinity in its ability to see the world and energetic world from all perspectives. For those of you who are psychic, any damage or slowing of energy movement through this chakra has a direct impact on your ability to communicate with the spirits. It is as though you are trying to see through a very heavy veil. Although you may be a phenomenal psychic, any blockages or slowing of energy through this center will affect your ability to receive or translate information from the souls trying to communicate with their loved ones. Some of the messages that get through are garbled, distorted, and hard to understand. This leads to a significant miscommunication between what the soul said and what the psychic understood from the communication. At times, this miscommunication leads to others doubting the authenticity of your abilities.

For everyone, blockages or slow energy movement through this chakra can make you feel lost or that you lack direction in your life. If you are in a troublesome situation and you are trying to find the right path to take, blockages make you feel as though you are lost in a maze; no matter where you turn, there is a wall blocking your progression that you cannot get past. Although you are searching for and seeking answers, you are confused about which path is the "right" one to take. This loss of direction makes some people feel that they need to grasp at any potential solution to a problem just to make some type of progress. However, these "solutions" may make the situation worse than before. This condition can lead to feelings of hopelessness, helplessness, or despair.

Blockages also cloud your vision of reality and can skew your perception, blocking you from seeing things or people as they really are instead of as what you wish for them to be. You can be blinded by circumstances or see only what others want you to focus on. In this respect, your third eye chakra functions in the same way as your brain. Your brain will ignore what it does not focus on as though it does not exist. The same phenomenon applies to your spirit body's ability to see. If your spirit body focuses too much on the microdetails of a situation, you might miss the big picture. This makes it difficult for you to put an event into perspective and to see the solution to your problems, even if the universe places the answer directly in front of you.

THROAT CHAKRA

Your throat chakra aligns with the physical location of the base of your throat. The color resonance is light blue, which aligns with the energy of communication. This chakra promotes your ability to hear others and to speak your truth. The throat chakra infuses your human trinity with inner power to say what you think or have learned. This is where your human trinity has the energy to speak with the strength of conviction and confidence in sharing your truth. Through it, you can communicate what your angels, guides, or the universe has shared with you. From this chakra energy, you can also share information from souls who have passed and have messages for loved ones who are still in the human trinity form. When energy is moving through this chakra very quickly, your speed of communicating with others can become extremely fast and hard for others to follow.

This is the chakra most powerfully affected when you do any type of public speaking. When the energy is flowing freely, you believe that others are valuing the information you are sharing. Whenever there is a slowing of energy or a blockage, there are usually communication issues within both your physical and spirit bodies. In your physical body, you are limited in your ability to speak your truth. From your spirit body's perspective, you might feel fearful of sharing what you think, worrying that others may not like it or that it will have no value. This fear can leave your physical being feeling paralyzed as you try to speak, stutter, or stammer, or sound afraid as you speak. If the blockage is the result of trying to share information through public speaking of some type, the energy from those around you is affecting you. Essentially, it is as though their collective energy has placed a choke hold on your throat chakra and is squeezing this chakra so tightly it is hard for you to communicate, and at times even to physically speak.

For those of us who are not public speakers, this choke hold on our chakra is no less powerful. It may lead to a loss of ability to voice your basic needs or wants in an appropriate manner. You might feel so constricted that you need to raise a lot of energy within your spirit body to speak your truth. However, once the energy moves, it can be fast and a little uncontrolled. As a result, you could end up overexpressing your needs in an exaggerated way that seems overblown for a situation. It can give you the title of being somewhat overemotional. This can become very frustrating because your message of how you are feeling is trivialized as an emotional outburst and little if anything happens to resolve the issue. Energy blockages in this center also make it difficult for you to communicate the information received from others or from the divine. Even though the information sent was clear, when you try to share it with others, you struggle to find the "right" words to share the message without changing the intent. You might focus so intently on finding the words that the essence of the message is lost or you may forget part of the message.

HEART CHAKRA

The heart chakra is located in the middle of the chest around the location of the physical heart. The color resonance is green or pink. Your heart chakra is your love energy center. This includes loving oneself as well as loving others. People with energy that resonates as green from this chakra tend to keep their heart open to new thoughts, ideas, or ways of thinking or being. When this chakra has a green resonance, it may be that people are actively trying to pull in positive feelings of happiness or love in their lives. However, it also might be green because they love money and they are trying to draw in more of it into their lives.

Many people have pink energy resonating from this chakra. However, the color differs depending on how people process love energy through their spirit body. When the heart chakra resonates with light pink energy, people tend to be open to love in its different forms. At times, their interpretation or definition of what love is or "looks like" differs dramatically from that of others around them and is changeable. The color dark pink suggests that they are an incurable romantic or have strong defined preconceptions of what love looks and feels like.

It could also mean that the person may be struggling to find love or to believe others love them. The color fuchsia suggests that people are looking for love and view everyone they meet in the best light while ignoring some of their negative qualities. If the chakra energy is varying shades of pink in circles within this chakra and the energy is darker the closer you get to the center of the chakra, it suggests that the person is very understanding and forgives easily. They like to draw people to themselves. Even though they have preconceived ideas of what love should be like, they apply those rules to themselves but rarely to others. As a side note, some people's chakras resonate with a pink center surrounded with a green energy resonance. It is quite beautiful to see. These individuals demonstrate energetic characteristics of both green and pink energy centers.

Regardless of what color it resonates, this center is fundamental to your personal healing and gives you the ability to draw in healing energy from the universal energy grid. Through this chakra, we also project to others who we believe ourselves to be. You send out healing energy to others through this chakra. If you have emotional hurts, this is the energy center that clogs with residual energy from them. Through this chakra, you embrace your faith and beliefs about what is true or right, and when the energy is strong, it corresponds to strong feelings of passion and commitment to your beliefs. This is also the chakra through which your spirit body sustains trust in others or humanity. If they break your trust, your heart chakra energy can ache, leaving your physical body feeling a sense of loss or sadness.

Whenever there is damage to your heart chakra, your ability to give and receive love is affected. Damage or sluggish energy movement affects your ability to accept and love yourself. It is difficult to send out love energy to another when you do not have very much love energy in this chakra to sustain yourself. This condition may lead people to think they are worthless or that they do not deserve to love. Others are willing to settle for whatever crumb of love they can find just to be with someone, even if the person is not very nice to them. When the energy is slow or has blockages, even though you know you love someone, you might feel almost apathetic toward him or her, or you feel nothing at all. If you are in this phase, it might feel like you are looking in on someone else's life. It may even feel as though you are a bystander in your own world and do not even understand why you are feeling so empty.

SOLAR PLEXUS/WILL CHAKRA

The solar plexus, or "will" chakra, aligns with the physical location between the navel and the bottom tip of the sternum. It aligns anywhere higher or lower within this location depending on your spirit body and its density. The color resonance is yellow and ranges from a very pale yellow to a dark yellow hue. Typically, the darker the yellow, the stronger you are in enacting your will within your life. However, a yellow/brown color indicates that you are acting out the will of another within your life or there is some type of energy blockage through this chakra.

Essentially, the power through this chakra allows you to take charge of your life and decide on what you want to happen, and then having the strength of will to make it happen. From this chakra comes your determination to succeed or overcome obstacles that are blocking you from achieving your goals. It gives you the undeniable sense that you have the power to enact change in your life and make your dreams come true. The energy flowing through this chakra fills your spirit body with determination and establishes the boundaries of what you are willing to do or put up with from others.

This chakra contributes energy that defines and shares your personal wisdom and knowledge through your human trinity, giving you a gut feeling on how to proceed. At times, the energy within this center is your first warning that you should consider proceeding with caution. This inner wisdom guides you and helps you figure out how you will use your personal power to enact change within your life. The energy center affects your will to live out your soul's right to practice its own free will. This energy center manifests what you believe to be true about yourself. It is also the part of your spirit body that writes the essence of your life's experience on your soul.

Whenever there is damage or a slowing of energy movement through the solar plexus/will chakra, your spirit body loses clarity or direction, and may become vulnerable to the influences of others. This is because when your spirit body feels lost or feels that it does not know the best course of action, your human trinity will look outward to find direction. At times, a reduction of energy leaves you feeling fearful and uncertain that you have the ability to manifest your goals and dreams in life. This includes manifesting your desires and wishes to improve your life, even though they would not harm another. You might feel as though you have no idea on how to proceed or how to begin moving past a situation or hurt.

At times, the temporary blockage in energy movement is due to an energy strike to this chakra. Any type of attack in this area of your spirit body will make you feel like you have just been sucker punched. If you sustain an energy strike or attack, it will cause the energy to rush out of the chakras above and below it simultaneously due to the force, making your spirit body feel as though it is gasping for energy. This situation creates a mini vacuum within your spirit body until you pull in new energy from the universe to replenish the energy you lost due to the attack. Some people feel like they cannot move energy in any direction within their spirit body for a short period until the impact of the energy strike passes.

SACRAL CHAKRA

The physical alignment of your spirit body's sacral chakra is in your lower abdomen. The color resonance of this chakra is orange. Similar to the other chakras, this color resonance varies in hue depending on energy movement. If someone has a weak energy flow through this chakra, the energy resonates as a very light orange. The stronger the energy force, the darker and richer the orange hue becomes. Whenever any other color resonance leaks through, this indicates some type of blockage or an overabundance of energy running through this chakra. If it is an orange-red color, then the chakra is having difficulty handling large volumes of energy rushing up from the base chakra.

Your sacral chakra is your power source, giving you a sense of entitlement to live out your life goals and a feeling that you deserve to have good things happen in your life. This chakra also serves as your pleasure energy and is responsible for managing your sex energy. We manifest our physical body's desires through this chakra. As the second chakra from the base of your spirit body, it has the ability to draw in healing energy and translate it into the form of personal healing that your spirit body or physical body requires.

Damage to this center or a slowing of energy movement could leave you doubting that you deserve to have happiness or joy in your life. There is always some loss of personal power when there is an energetic restriction through this chakra. As your second chakra, if energy cannot move through it well, it has a direct effect on the energy received by the remaining five chakras above it. Energy reductions passing through this chakra may result in the affected person devaluing themselves. Some subjugate personal needs to satisfy the needs of others to their own detriment. They may not feel that their wants or needs are valid in respect to the wants or needs of others. At other times, they may belittle their own contributions or value to themselves, others, or humanity.

Slow energy or blockages in this chakra can cause a sense of depression within the spirit body that transfers to the physical body for processing. Whenever anything suppresses sacral energy, it creates suction of energy within your spirit body and pulls energy down from the upper chakras toward it. This contributes to a feeling of being "down" or sad. Even though you are trying hard to send energy upward, it is tough to raise the energy through the chakras. Reduction of energy can have impacts on an individual's sexuality as well. When energy is reduced through this chakra, people may find that their sexual desires and drives also diminish. Conversely, they might try to fill up this chakra with energy from others in their attempt to pull themselves out of the sadness or emptiness they feel.

ROOT/BASE CHAKRA

This chakra aligns with the physical end of your tailbone. The color resonance associated with this chakra is red. The energy resonance is that of strength, power, and grounding. Your taproot that reaches out from your spirit body connects you at your base chakra to the universal energy grid. This is a primary connection to the divine energy of all life and is your safety rope to cling to when life gets crazy or is pushing you around. Your root is also the power center of your spirit body. Do not confuse this with the soul. Your soul is the power center of your human trinity. Through your root, you can draw significant energy to push through your spirit body as you reach to the divine through your crown chakra.

Grounding your energy provides your spirit body with a sense of stability and permanence. Not only is this chakra critical for grounding, it is also a primary source used to draw energy from the universal energy grid into your spirit body. If you lose your connection from your taproot to the universal energy grid, you have cut off a primary source that nourishes your spirit body. It would be similar to going on a crash diet in your physical being and refusing to eat or drink anything for a long period. If you do not restore your nutrition and hydration in time, this can result in significant damage within the physical body that can result in death. Energy from the universal energy grid is the same as nutrition and hydration for the physical body. From a spirit body perspective, the energy received through the root chakra and taproot is critical for survival of your human trinity.

This multi-action chakra is one of the chakras responsible for nourishing your spirit body with new, refreshed energy, allowing it to "breathe." Additionally, it has the function of expelling residual energy caught up in the spirit body back to the grid for recycling. By organically grounding your spirit body through your taproot, you lessen the chance that the residual energy in your spirit body will reach toxic levels that affect energy movement within the entire spirit body.

When this energy center is damaged, or if energy movement becomes sluggish, the very first impact is your sense of stability in your life. You might feel unsettled or anxious. If another has betrayed you, this damages this chakra, profoundly affecting your ability to trust others. Interestingly, if energy is blocked, it sometimes appears that the person is well grounded. The reason for this is that all of the spirit body energy is stuck around the root chakra. However, the clue that you are stuck and not grounded is that when you are grounding well, your energy cycles through your spirit body and expels old energy out of the base chakra. If the energy is stuck, your energy is not moving well into any of the chakras above the base chakra. The rest of your spirit body is starving from the lack of energy, leaving your human trinity feeling almost lethargic and tired. It is like going on a crash diet that is so restrictive you are not getting enough calories to keep your physical body functioning well. Although your spirit body does not give off hunger pains like the physical body, it does create a huge void within you that your physical body will try to fill. This void may lead to some type of addictive behavior that gives short-term pleasure but only leaves you feeling just as empty as before.

THE SONA—THE EIGHTH CHAKRA

I believe there are eight chakras. Although there is no generally accepted view of this eighth chakra, I believe that it is associated with living out your soul's purpose and is your "sona." As I mentioned earlier in this book, your spirit body connects to your soul and physical body through the sona. Your sona is the integral connection that holds your human trinity in a single functioning unit. It is the primary source of energy that awakens your human trinity to life in the physical form. This connection is usually found around the area of your heart chakra. However, if you are going through an "energetic earthquake" in your life, you might feel pain around the area of your sona.

Your sona connects your human trinity of the physical body, spirit body, and soul. It is the most powerful energy center in your human trinity, sustaining your human life form. As the energy center housing your soul, it has a direct link to the divine, an incredibly strong source of energy. You soul gives you the strength to keep going even when your world crashes around you. The word *sona* loosely translates to "Orion's belt." Just as Orion's belt points to Sirius, which some believe to be the source of life, the sona houses the source of life within our human trinity. Through this energy mechanism, your soul drives energy through your chakras, spirit body, and physical body simultaneously. Like the serpentine belt in a vehicle, your sona drives energy in a primary direction. When it is moving in this direction, you cannot feel the movement. It is like standing outside. Although the earth is spinning fast, unless the ground is shaking, we cannot feel it moving. However, if the earth starts shaking hard due to an earthquake or an explosion, we can. The same premise applies to your sona. Unless something happens and your sona experiences the equivalent of an energetic earthquake, or a disruption of energy movement, you are probably unaware of its presence. If you sustain significant damage to the sona that it opens, it allows your soul to permanently disconnect from the physical and spirit bodies causing death to the human trinity.

Not only does this energy center drive energy through your human trinity, it also allows you to live out your life's purpose. It circulates your energy through your spirit body much like your bloodstream sends nutrients through your physical body and carries the waste from your tissues and organs and removes it from your body. Your sona dictates the overall direction of energy that your spirit moves within your spirit body. The main purpose of the sona is to connect our three forms of existence into a single human form where your soul lives out its life's mandate. Rarely does anyone ever connect to your sona. It has divine protection since it is the essence of who you are. Any connections to it are detrimental to your existence. Therefore, your soul will rebel if anyone tries to connect to it.

Chapter 3

TWO-WAY COMMUNICATION NETWORK

Many of you reading this book have a good idea of how your emotions and physical body interact. How your spirit body and physical body communicate with each other may not be as clear to you. As I mentioned earlier in this book, your spirit body superimposes on your physical body and has the ability to act alone or in tandem with your physical body. Through this connection, you function as a human trinity where your soul provides the spark of life-sustaining energy. As a result of this deeply embedded connection, your physical body and spirit body have the ability to act as one. Although your sona tethers your human trinity into a single entity, your spirit body uses the brain stem to send messages to the physical body. This is the core of the highly effective and efficient two-way communication network between your spirit body and your physical body. This connection allows your physical body and spirit body to communicate freely. It is why we can hear our inner voice and the messages that our soul is sending out into our human trinity. As you process information in your brain, it shares the information with your spirit body and vice versa. This sharing gives you the ability to process information in a multidimensional way.

This multidimensional processing is why your brain gives you one answer, but your spirit body may give a completely different answer. Your spirit body's messages are often translated by your brain as "gut feelings" on how to proceed. The reason for this is that the brain tries to make sense of the "facts" and categorize the information it receives into a form it can rationalize. If people have a fundamental belief that all answers must be based on fact, or on what they can see, hear, feel, taste, or touch, their brain often discounts the information from the spirit body as secondary or invalid. However, if someone's brain is predominant and discounts information from the spirit body, it doesn't necessarily mean that the "physical answer" resulting from the brain's data processing is more correct. Rather, it may just be that your brain believes that only answers based on physical data where there are concrete facts to back them up indicate the right approach. If you are one who tends to go with facts over feelings, your soul may have been deceived in a past life, with catastrophic results. Your soul may be less willing to accept anything unless it can be proved. Regardless of what you decide to do, there may not be a single "right" answer. Rather, these diverging opinions are sometimes just different ideas on how to proceed.

The reality is that our brains can attend to only a limited amount of data. Your brain's job is to make sense of what is going on around you. It tends to rely on external cues to determine what is relevant and what isn't. Every second it is bombarded with huge volumes of data. There is no way that it can capture and categorize every piece of data. Instead, it selectively filters information and tries to hold onto the information it deems important. Then it takes the information that it has captured, reviews it, categorizes it, and files it away in your memory, depending on what the brain is focusing on at the moment. Information it is working on is in your short-term memory. If your brain decides it is important, or if you take the time to memorize the information, only then can it move into your long-term memory. Unfortunately, due to our brain's selective process, even when we are looking directly at something, our brains can dismiss or completely ignore important information. This is especially true if the brain is focusing very closely on something like a magic trick. While magicians have you focus on some type of focal point, such as a deck of cards or a hat, they are doing other things to make the trick "work." However, your brain doesn't even notice it. It is so busy paying attention to something, trying to make sense of what you are seeing that it ignores the sleight of hand that is occurring.

However, some people trust their "gut" over the course of action suggested by their brain. Whenever people trust their spirit body's assessment of what to do next, it doesn't mean that they are completely dismissing what their brain thinks. Rather, they may have experienced situations where they did or did not listen to their spirit body, and it turned out that if they had followed their intuition, the outcome would have been better for them. As a result, they believe that their spirit body has their highest good in mind. However, depending on the connections you share with others, what others tell you or how your brain interprets the information and shares the results with your spirit body, the message can be skewed.

The connection between your spirit body and physical body is very strong, even if you find you value logic and reason over what your gut feelings suggest you should be doing. Regardless of whether you go with your gut or your head, there is a real chance that you will misinterpret the information. The beauty of our human trinity is that it gives us the ability to consider everything from both perspectives before we make a decision. It also gives us the ability to create a unique approach that is a blend of the courses of action that your brain and spirit body have offered. Sometimes, the answer we choose is based the elements that our spirit body and brains both agree on. However, as hard as we try to make the "right" decision, we cannot always predict how another will react. Regardless of the decision you make, another's interpretation of, or reaction to your decision can affect the outcome in a way you did not expect. So, even though you made a "good" decision, depending on what others do, it sometimes ends up that it was not the best course of action for that specific situation.

I personally find it fascinating how our spirit body communicates with the physical body and vice versa. These entities connect intimately at two points. The first is the sona, which sustains your human trinity with energy. This connection is fundamental to the survival of your human trinity. Without the energy from your soul coursing through your human trinity, infusing it with your essence of being, you would die. However, through the sona your human trinity gains a basic will to live and survive. The second point is at our brain stem. As I explain how this works, I use the word "brain" loosely. There are different parts of your brain that handles differing aspects of the electronic impulses from your physical and spirit bodies. Rather than turn this into a biology lesson, I am simplifying all brain functions as simply, 'the brain' or 'the brain stem'. At your brain stem is where your spirit body's energy from the throat chakra communicates with your physical body. At this point, it connects with your physical body's brain and central nervous system which is responsible for processing all of the information received from both your physical body and your spirit body.

From an energetic perspective, our central nervous system illustrates the complexity of energy movement within our physical body and the amazing sophistication of our human body as a machine. As I explain how this works from a physical perspective, there also are corresponding movements of energy within your spirit body. From a very general perspective, once the information is received from your spirit body by your physical body, it communicates the information to your brain. From there, your brain sends a message to the peripheral nervous system within your physical body, putting it on alert. This state sends a message to your central nervous system to process the incoming information and to elicit a response or sensation within the physical body. Since the physical and spirit bodies are superimposed on each other, the physical body tends to feel the message in the area that corresponds to where the message originated within the spirit body.

Depending on the message received, your physical body will feel at peace or different areas of your physical body will be activated, providing information on how your spirit body was affected. If your spirit body was struck by the negative energy of another, these feelings of injury can be so strong that it feels like your actual physical body has been struck or burnt. Since your physical body and spirit body are in constant communication, they will inform each other when they need to act. It is amazing how a blow to your spirit body is manifested as sensations in the same area of your physical body.

You are probably wondering how your spirit body can manifest feelings or sensations in your physical body. The explanation is linked to the involuntary and voluntary responses of your nervous system. For the purpose of simplifying how your spirit body communicates with your physical body and vice versa, I will focus on the involuntary responses elicited by energy blows or pending energy strikes against your human trinity.

Once your spirit body has detected any type of energetic shift or a blow, it sends pulses of energy with messages of what has happened to the area within your spirit body, up through the closest chakra, and up through each subsequent chakra to the throat chakra. From here, the energetic messages are directed to the top of the spinal cord and into your brain stem. Once the message is received, the brain begins to process the information. At the same time, it activates your central nervous system and sends a message to the corresponding physical organ or location in the body where there has been an energy strike or impending strike on the spirit body. This also applies if negative energy is gathering in the cosmos and threatening to strike your human trinity.

Regardless of whether the energy is calming or a warning, the spirit body elicits a response from the physical body that informs your brain of what is happening from the energetic perspective ... which, of course, your brain translates, reformats, and tries to understand. If a physical response resolves the issue, your spirit body will use the autonomic nervous system to stimulate organs to increase or decrease functionality. In tandem, this causes sensations in your physical body.

By sending a message to your brain, your spirit body is essentially putting your physical body on notice that it might need to defend itself from some type of looming threat or that an event that will affect you is on its way. If you have a feeling of foreboding or fear, you tend to pay closer attention to the environment around you to assess the potential threat to your physical being. The same applies to pending energy strikes to your spirit body. Even though no one is actively sending the energy directly at you, the universe detects it and sends a warning to your spirit body through the universal energy grid that energy is building against your or that another is wishing ill on you. However, there are times when this energy is simply the result of your guides or angels trying to communicate with you.

What I find to be the strangest thing about this phenomenon is that your physical body feels perfectly fine at one moment. Emotionally, you may even feel quite calm and peaceful and be going about your life feeling happy and content. The next moment, you are feeling anything but calm or peaceful. In fact, your physical being is telling you that something just happened or is about to happen. Interestingly enough, we tend to pay more attention to the sudden onset of anxious energy over a burst of optimism or happiness. Regardless, if you are suddenly feeling anxious or calm, you may not even know why you are feeling this way. How your spirit body manifests sensations in your physical body gives you a glimpse into the intent of the energy that is either building in the cosmos or the energy that is being thrown directly at your human trinity. If the injury is due to an energy attack and your spirit body is injured, damaged, or struggling to move energy or draw in energy, it lets the physical body know that something is wrong. It is interesting that when the spirit body shares information on where it was injured, your physical body sometimes translates the message into pain or hurt within the physical body in the area corresponding to the position within the spirit body.

Remember, your spirit body doesn't only send messages of an impending energy strike or a looming threat. It also notifies you when something has happened in the cosmos that means things are going to be improving in your life. You might have been asking for divine assistance or for guidance. Sometimes the energy received is soothing to your spirit body and calms it. In this case, your spirit body sends a pulse of energy to your brain stem, which stimulates the physical body to release a feeling of peace in your physical being. It also triggers a "knowing" that everything is going to be fine. At this point, your body triggers responses that reduce stress in your physical body. Whenever you feel this, be sure to send thanks to the divine.

Your physical body also has the ability to communicate with the spirit body. As your brain processes information, it also sends messages to your spirit body through the brain stem into the throat chakra. In this communication, the brain shares critical information regarding the impact the event has had on the physical body. From here, the information goes through all chakras within the spirit body to process the information to assess whether there is corresponding damage from energy attacks within it. If the flood of messages is significant, some of the information is discounted by your brain as "unimportant" before sending the message into your spirit body to focus on the data it thinks are relevant to the situation. This is the time when I personally feel that everything becomes almost surreal. Although the events are moving fast, it suddenly feels as though you are in slow motion as the events continue to unfold. Regardless of the severity of a situation, as long as your brain is awake, it assesses what is happening to the physical and spirit bodies to determine how your human trinity feels about the situation. Using all of the information that your brain feels is relevant, a decision is made on your human trinity's course of action.

Depending on the emotions the physical body is releasing from the brain, the spirit body tries to relate the emotions and energy swirling through it as a result of the physical impact with the severity of the hurt or happiness that the physical body reports it has sustained. At this point, the spirit body accesses the Akashic records to determine if this is a life-or-death situation in which your soul is going to choose whether to check out of this lifetime. Using this information, the spirit body starts formulating a plan for sustaining itself. This information is shared back to the brain stem for processing. Throughout this communication, the spirit body is very aware of what is happening in the physical body.

If the injury is traumatic and the physical body loses consciousness, you may have an out-of-body experience. Essentially, your brain is still sharing what it can about what is happening to the physical body but at a reduced pace, but your spirit body is still active and alert. In this state, when your brain is no longer sending signals to the spirit body on how it feels, the spirit body cannot sense the pain. During out-of-body experiences, you won't feel anything other than a strange numbness or nothingness, even though you are aware of what is happening around or to your physical body. At times, this can include you looking down on your physical body and hearing what is being said and watching what others are doing. During this time you may even find that your spirit body tells your physical body that it must wake up, or you may have a sense that if something doesn't change quickly, you might die. For some, this is when they hear their guardian angel telling them they need to stay, that their loved ones still need them.

When your physical body eventually awakes, your spirit body informs your brain of what transpired in what is sometimes an abbreviated short story. It typically does not provide all of the information if it thinks that your brain cannot handle the information right away. Even when it does, your brain will choose whether or not it retains the information and passes it into your conscious mind as a memory. If your brain doesn't think you can handle the full outline of events, it will block those memories, possibly forever. Unfortunately, this process just stuffs down the energy into residual energy deep within your spirit body, which can have negative consequences for your human trinity.

This extreme example illustrates how our spirit body becomes an onlooker when physical trauma is occurring that temporarily incapacitates the physical body. When it is due to injury or a traumatic event, even if your physical body cannot handle the memories or the events unfolding, you spirit body can, and it does. It is always alert and present in every situation, even when your physical body is not. It is the part of us that never sleeps. This is the part of us that can cause insomnia in our physical bodies when energy is swirling within us and we are struggling to calm ourselves. Although you may not physically remember all of the details of an event, any traumatic event leaves behind energy residue within your spirit body. In this case, it is the waste product of your spirit body drawing in new energy, while some of its energy was depleted as it continued to interface with your physical body, even when the physical body temporarily stopped taking in new messages. Depending on what has occurred, your spirit body might share what you have learned from the experience with your soul, where it is recorded and becomes part of your Akashic records.

Blessedly, most events in your life are not so traumatic to the physical body that it is temporarily incapacitated and your brain slows down or ceases to communicate with your spirit body—leaving your spirit body as the only consciousness you can access. Even if the physical body is active, if your spirit body becomes the predominant essence of your human trinity, there is always a feeling of detachment from what is unfolding. Your soul also becomes a bystander "watching" the events.

This may be due to the spirit body failing to immediately share with your brain how it is feeling or what it is experiencing during the events, or it could be sharing information, but your brain is overwhelmed with the volume of data it is receiving. Regardless of the cause, your brain processes the physical information first, since its survival is critical to the human trinity, and then it processes the spirit body and soul information later. As it begins to receive the spirit body messages, including those the spirit body is passing along from the soul once the physical threat has passed, it throws your human trinity into shock. Literally, your spirit body becomes very chatty and uses up so much of your brain's processing power that it partially detaches from the physical world as it reviews the incoming information for any additional information it needs to sustain your human trinity.

If the physical trauma was the result of someone actually hitting you, your physical body's response may be to hit the person back. However, your spirit body might be telling your brain to drop your fist that it isn't worth causing you ethical or legal issues for a moment of physical release. This situation leaves your brain in a dilemma. It is being fed copious amounts of adrenaline, and the fight-or-flight response is running high. Where the physical body wants to fight, it is waging an internal battle with the spirit body, which wants the physical body to turn off this response. In this situation, when people step away from a fight rather than retaliating, their spirit body has successfully convinced the physical body that physical violence is not the best way to resolve the issue.

Conversely, if you are in a life or death situation, or you need to protect your human trinity from some horrible fate, both your physical body and your spirit body will push for the fight response if escaping the threat is not an option. The threat can be external or internal in the form of a disease that is destroying the physical body, such as cancer. It is the responsibility of your spirit body to notify the human trinity if the Akashic records show that it must fight in order to survive or whether your soul is getting ready to leave. Even if you are not aware that you are accessing the Akashic records, in these situations it presents as a deep-seated, overwhelming belief of what is going to happen. Depending upon the situation, you may find that a deep well of energy opens upon within you making you stronger than you have ever felt before. Thankfully, you may never experience a situation in which you are in dire circumstances and your physical being is in some type of immediate jeopardy. The important thing to remember is that in our daily lives, our spirit body is in communication with the physical body and vice versa on a constant basis.

It is amazing how effectively and efficiently our physical body and spirit body communicate with each other. Every day, our physical body manifests symptoms, sensations or feelings that originate within our spirit body. Using the energy within your spirit body, it can generate similar feelings within the physical body through the two-way communication network. On a daily basis, our physical body continually tells us how our spirit body is doing. You might feel butterflies in your tummy when your spirit body is feeling nervous or excited about something. At times, you may even feel like a part of your body had just been scorched after your spirit body sustained a direct hit of energy that hurt it. You might even feel sharp shooting pain in a shoulder or your back that quickly passes; this pain may be the result of someone "stabbing you in the back" with a verbal attack even though you had no knowledge he or she was doing it. Your spirit body puts your physical body on notice if swirling energy in the cosmos is directed at your human trinity regardless of whether it is good or bad. Essentially, it lets your physical body know that there is going to be a shift in your world. Remember, your spirit body can reach to the universe for divine information at any time it chooses. When it receives this information, it shares it with the physical body.

When our spirit body has swirling energy within its trunk, we get a churning or anxious feeling within our physical trunk. At times, significant movement of energy through your spirit body can result in your physical body having "energy motion sickness." This condition starts with you moving large quantities of energy through your spirit body due to swirling energy, or when you are drawing energy from another person who is spinning. If it's the result of moving a lot of energy from another, your spirit body is left feeling energetically "light headed." It notifies your physical body that your energy in your spirit body is off balance and it is feeling unwell. Depending on where you process the energy and where the pockets of energy residue within your spirit body have consolidated, what happens differs.

If it consolidates in your stomach or small intestine, your physical body interprets the message that your spirit body has energy motion sickness and needs to purge what is causing the energetic imbalance. Then, in its attempt to rid your spirit body of the concentrated energy residue, the physical body displays symptoms of "energy sickness". This feels similarly to being sick with a stomach bug. You will feel nauseated and feel like you are going to vomit. In fact, if the energy movement or swirling energy causing the energy motion sickness is significant, there is a very good chance that you will be physically sick. Happily, though, the symptoms from energy motion sickness tend to pass after a few hours. You will know this is due to energy since you can feel the energy swirling within your spirit body. Once the swirling eases, the feeling of physical sickness immediately passes.

If the energy was processed through the lower trunk of your spirit body, and the residual energy becomes concentrated there, your physical body interprets the message as your spirit body is congested and needs to purge this energy buildup. The result is that you can end up with "energy cramps." Your physical body responds by stimulating your bowels to release whatever is in them. This process manifests as cramps in your lower abdominal area, loose stools, or even diarrhea, depending on the strength of the energy movement and the concentration of residual energy. For some of you, this diarrhea can be almost explosive as it leaves your physical body. If the energy is spinning hard in your spirit body, or if you have a chameleon spirit body, you can have both "energy sickness" and "energy cramps" simultaneously. I am always amazed how quickly the physical body responds to significant energy movement within the spirit body in its attempt to return homeostasis to the human trinity. Unfortunately, the only way to speed up the process of recovery from energy motion sickness or energy cramps is to meditate to quiet your energy and draw in new refreshed energy from the universal energy grid. I find meditating with a Septarian stone is very helpful. The Septarian stone meditation I use can be found in my book *Taking Back Your Joy of Living*.

Your spirit body also reacts as it receives energy from your physical body. When your physical body tells your spirit body that something is not "right" within it, your spirit body investigates. This is when you "know' something is wrong but may not even be sure what it is. This gives you the opportunity to seek out medical help to figure out what is wrong and how to manage or solve the problem. Whenever we are open to the messages from both our physical and spirit bodies, it allows us to function as the highly sophisticated human trinity we were designed to be. If we choose to ignore our spirit bodies and rely heavily on our physical body, our human trinity becomes unbalanced. Then, when difficult circumstances enter your life, it is much more difficult to navigate through them and keep a sense of peace, believing that everything will eventually be okay and you will get through the troublesome life stage. Although your physical body is the machine through which you act out your life, your spirit body can provide you with important navigational information that can help you avoid some of life's pitfalls. If can also infuse your being with hope and a sense of peace.

The interconnection between the spirit body and the physical body is so strong that if your spirit body is full of angst resulting from difficult life events, symptoms can manifest in your physical body. Such symptoms can include pain, cognitive difficulties, panic disorders, or even difficulty making life decisions. Whenever your spirit body is injured, and you stuff down the resulting residual energy resulting from the hurt and pain instead of working through it, this can create a temporary plug in your spirit body. This plug can temporarily stop the "bleed" of energy from it. However, when incoming energy disturbs the residual energy, it causes the energy within you to swirl and become chaotic. This can disturb the residual energy plug in your spirit body and move the energy, only to expose a gaping hole with energy flows out of and back into the cosmos. In turn, your spirit body sends the message to your physical body that it is bleeding and injured. Your brain interprets this information that your spirit body is injured. Then your physical body manifests pain the same area where your spirit body is losing energy.

The unfortunate outcome is that if your spirit body is weeping energy and in pain and you cannot find a corresponding injury in your physical body, you may think that the pain is in your head. However, the pain is very real. When there is genuinely no physical reason for pain in your body, this suggests that the pain is in your spirit body where medications and physical therapy cannot reach it to promote healing or numb the pain. This may be the reason that you do not get relief from a pain medication, treatment plans and therapy prescribed by medical doctors or other practitioners for your physical condition doesn't seem to be working. To heal, you need to do some deep work on your spirit body to promote healing. Unfortunately, there is no magic pill that is going to remove the residual energy that is causing you pain, seal up the wound, and restore the energy within you.

Whenever you receive information from the physical body versus the spirit body, it is a challenge to figure out which body is processing the information and supplying additional data. Your question is probably, "How do I know?" From a general perspective, your brain provides the logic around the information or some type of order to the information. Your spirit body provides the response of how it feels about the situation. At times, some of the angst you are feeling is due to residual energy being stirred up, and old feelings and emotions infusing your human trinity. Your soul provides insight on what it thinks is the best course of action depending on what it has learned from your current and prior lifetimes. In essence, your human trinity is responding to the old situation and the new situation at the same time. When this happens, it can cause your human trinity to spin temporarily as it tries to reconcile what action it should take.

Chapter 4

THOUSANDS OF DEGREES OF CONNECTION

Through our spirit bodies, we have the divine ability to connect to each other to form our human relationship matrix. There is no mistaking that our soul is programmed to seek out the company of others to some degree. These connections can be critical supports when we are going through difficult life phases or struggle to draw energy into our spirit bodies. This support allows us to grow, experience love and have a sense of belonging in our human form. The umbilical cord connections we make with our loved ones are very strong; continuing even after the person you loved has died.

We are born into an existing human relationship energy matrix. This is composed of your family of origin, extended family, and family friends. For some people, the original human relationship matrix they have at birth is very small, while others are quite extensive. The degree of connectedness also depends on whether you directly connect to someone through one or more other people. Regardless of the size of your human relationship matrix at birth, throughout your life, people will join it and leave it. This is part of the natural progression of life.

Some of the shared connections we have are by choice, while others are not. Connections tend to be very tight and strong with loved ones and very close friends. Together, this network of love connections forms your human relationship matrix. Some of the shared connections you have are good and help you in your life's journey, while others may drain you of energy or are in some other way not in your best interest. Although you have a personal human relationship matrix, it really is a small subset of the overall human energy collective of a worldwide human relationship matrix. Everyone belongs to this collective. In it, some people have many connections, whereas others do not. Our interconnectedness gives us the ability to send love, peace, hope, or any other positive form of energy to people we may never meet. We start by sending it through our connections, and it zooms over the collective until it reaches its intended destination. Think of it as the telecommunication network in which we pick up a phone and our voice goes through fiber-optic cables until it reaches the person we called, who could be on the other side of the world. Through this connection, we share energy with others through our voice.

It is similar to our umbilical cord connections. Through them, we give and receive energy. There are times when we give more than we get. Over time, in every healthy relationship, it balances out. Depending on how tightly you connect to people and their connectedness to others, you may sense energy of secondary or tertiary connections through your cords. Some matrixes are very tight and strong, which translates into an increased ability to send and receive energy for many more people than those to whom you directly connect. As people die, the ball of light in the matrix that was their spirit body goes out and they leave the human relationship matrix, creating a hole in it. If they were the only person holding a group of people together, the interconnectedness of the group disintegrates. You can sometimes see this in families when the matriarch or patriarch of the family dies and the entire family unit seems to implode, only for the members to drift apart and rarely have anything to do with each other.

You probably have heard that there are six degrees of connection to others. In the human relationship matrix, it is more like hundreds of thousands of degrees of connection, where eventually each of us connects to everyone else through someone else. This connection spans race, creed, religion, or any other way we define ourselves. It does not even matter if you strongly dislike someone. Eventually, we all connect through the human relationship matrix. Just like we all breathe air, we all draw energy from the universal energy grid and send and receive energy from others—either directly through a cord connection, or as points of energy shot from one end of the human relationship matrix to the other.

Connections start with primary connections. These are the umbilical cord connections that connect directly from your spirit body to the spirit body of another. Secondary connections are those that your primary connections have with others, but are not directly connected to you. Connections through a secondary connection that are not directly connected to you or your primary connections are tertiary connections and so on. Eventually, everyone's human relationship matrix connects to others and forms a global matrix including all members of humanity. Energetically, each person in the human relationship matrix is a point of energy. Then, with each connection, we have fine silvery connections to others we directly connect to in our matrix. They also have connections to their other primary connections, and so on. I have illustrated what this looks like from an energetic perspective in image 2.

Let us consider the following image from the perspective of our spirit body and our connections to others. The central sphere in this image represents your spirit body.

Image 2: Representation of your connections to
others in the human relationship matrix.

Each arm with single or multiple connections is an umbilical cord connection to another. The threads of energy that terminate in the cosmos are leakages in the cords due to poor maintenance of those connections or severed connections. Threads that connect two cords represent secondary connections, where you connect directly to someone as well as their connecting to another. At times, it can feel like there are three or more people in a relationship. Where a connection splits into two, this represents multiple connections to other's spirit body that originate from a single chakra connection to your spirit body. Each main branch of energy attaches to the spirit body of another.

CONNECTING TO OTHERS

Even after a loved one passes, the residual cord connections keep them close as they continue to watch us live our lives; many even cheer us on when we are going through a difficult life phase. It also allows them to send messages of love and remind us that they are still there for us. For me, my deceased loved ones even pop through just to chat about anything and nothing. At times, they want to remind me of a memory, check up on someone, or pass a message on to someone else. Sometimes, their message is simply to remind me to play and have fun when I am working too hard. Other times, they come through to remind me to share what I know with others. Anytime I find myself slacking off in writing a book, my grandmother is very quick to remind me that I need to help others as the angels have helped me. I have to admit, she can be very effective in reaching me at any time, night or day.

Although people leave the human relationship matrix through death, residual umbilical cord connections remain allowing you to stay connected. However, the ability to give and receive energy from the other is gone. You also lose the ability to connect to others through their secondary connections. Although a relationship matrix still exists, it connects from our human trinity plane of existence to the ethereal world that they inhabit after the loss of their human trinity. The reason for this is upon death, an automatic filter is installed by the universe and the umbilical cord connection transfers from the spirit body of the newly deceased to their soul. This maintains a relationship matrix connection, but crosses between two planes of existence. When both people have passed that shared a connection, the resulting connection is a soul-to-soul umbilical cord connection.

The beautiful thing about love cord connections is that they connect us to our soul group. Everyone belongs to a soul group of kindred spirits. These are people you have gone through life with before and chose to hang out with on the spirit side when you passed. When it was time to be born again, you chose to come back to life together. Within this group are friends, family members, and romantic partners. Depending on the person, they have been lucky and have had several romantic love matches. Even though they have drifted into a "friends only" relationship, the love bond persists. Some people focus on soul mates as the definitive measure of true love. There is a misconception that a soul mate is someone who is "just like you" ... almost as though he or she is your clone. However, I would be remiss if I didn't explain that true soul mates are the yin to your yang. Unfortunately, if you are really good with a little bad, they are mostly bad with a little bit of good. Depending on how "good" your "good" is, this can be a huge issue in your life if you connect with them. Consider this—if a woman was faith-filled, good, humble, put the needs of others before hers, gave to others until it hurt, her soul mate is most likely her direct opposite. As life partners, a 'soul mate' may detract from her life's mission if she was to use her kindness to help others, while her soul mate drew her to become more like them. From an energetic perspective, when soul mates are together in life, they balance out the energy they send out to the universe, making it neutral. If people are really, really good, that would mean their soul mates would need to be very, very bad to balance the energy.

Typically, the "best" relationships are between kindred spirits who are in your soul group. These are the people who are very similar to you and help you as you move through life's journey. If they are friends, the moment you met them you felt like you knew them "forever." You tend to have similar interests. However, they are not a "clone" of you in respect to likes and dislikes. Your resonance is similar and you may even have similar goals in life, even though the endgame results differ.

They tend to support you but also to challenge you to be your best. They can switch roles from a cheerleader to the person who will tell you the difficult truths, even when they know you do not want to hear what they have to say. These are the people with whom you can quickly share energy and who can send energy to you when it is needed. As part of your kindred soul group, they can help you to reconnect to each other in your human relationship matrix and quickly stabilize yourself if you have grown apart from members who no longer resonate in the same way you do. They also provide a stabilizing effect when you are losing members of your group that you relied upon for emotional or energetic support.

THE POWER OF THE MATRIX

The human relationship matrix is a very sophisticated energetic web of connections to which everyone in this world connects to form a massive matrix of energy. This human relationship matrix is a fundamental support system for our spirit body. Daily, life stresses or other factors can cause tears in our taproot, loosening its connection to the grid. The matrix can hold us and support us as we weather life's storms and provide us with a sense of belonging, love and stability. It also prevents our spirit bodies from drifting too far away from the universal energy grid and breaking this important connection. Our connections hold us in a flexible but firm energy net, and close to the universal energy grid as we try to reinforce our connection or reconnect to it.

Your human relationship matrix can be energetically as a flimsy as a spider's web or as strong as a high-quality trampoline. At first glance, you might think that this is a reflection of the number of people in your matrix. However, that is not necessarily true. The quality of the matrix is not dependent on the number of people to whom you connect; it is dependent on the strength of the connections you share with those connected directly to your spirit body. The tighter the connections and the healthier the energy transfers between you and to the people you connect to, the better it is for both of you. A few strong connections to people who are well grounded to the universal energy grid is far more effective than many connections to people with a weak connection to you or to the universal energy grid. You know you have a good matrix when it is strong enough to hold onto you when life is tough, but flexible enough to soften the impact of strong movements of energy that course through it.

The power from our human relationship matrix comes from our ability to easily move energy through it to share it or borrow it from others. Through these connections, even though we lose our way or our ability to draw energy into our spirit bodies from the universal energy grid is compromised, we still have a connection to this life-sustaining energy. As we go through life's struggles and it is tough to go on, those in your human matrix can choose to help you and encourage you to continue. Through their combined energy, they can help calm swirling energy within you and help you retain belief that the difficulty you are experiencing will eventually pass. They can also provide the motivation to not give up and to keep trying to achieve your dreams, hopes, or aspirations in life.

In many respects, the people in your human relationship matrix are like the stabilizers on a cruise ship that minimize the tilt of the boat in rough seas. On a ship, these are massive "fins" that extend from both sides of the ship and resemble the wings of a plane. Once they have been activated, even though the ship is still buffeted by the waves, the fins limit the chance that the ship will roll over in rough seas. Your connections in the human relationship matrix have a similar role. These connections stop you from "rolling over" energetically and giving up when you just need to hold on a little longer before your life storm ends. However, you need to let those in your matrix know you need their help and take the help when it is offered for it to be effective. If you consider the ship, even though it has stabilizers, if they are never activated, then they are useless in helping the ship stay upright in rough seas.

CHANGING CONNECTIONS

During your lifetime, you will experience several periods of transition when cord connections between yourself and loved ones seem to be dropping off. These transitions can begin as a slow atrophying of the cords, while at other times, it is as though someone has taken a machete and is cutting these cords faster than you can replace them. If you find that you are losing many people from your human relationship matrix, it is a sign that you or they are in periods of transformation. During this period, you are closing one life chapter in preparation for the next phase in your life. This change is never without pain, hurt, and at times, heartbreak. At times, this falling away of old connections is because they will hold you back from becoming who your soul desires to become in this lifetime. At times, this separation is part of a larger event decreed by fate. During major life transitions, you will find that some people who were once very close are more distant than before. Sometimes, this is a result of a change in resonance in which your spirit bodies begin to repel each other. Although these people were very important to you, somehow you have drifted apart while your soul's development was manifesting within your spirit body. The more people you lose as primary connections in your matrix, the more you will begin to feel somehow "disconnected." The loss of these cord connections can leave you feeling lost, alone, and powerless in the storm of life going on around you. It is more traumatic when you lose many cord connections within a short period.

We all mourn the loss of relationships in different ways. Some of these lost connections hurt more than others, leaving us wondering how we can ever move on. Not only have you lost a person as a part of your life, you have also lost the sense of connectedness you had when energy moved through the previously shared cord(s). If the relationship was once very strong and large volumes of energy moved between you, then losing it can feel traumatic or overwhelming. This is especially true if this was the primary way that you obtained new energy to nourish your spirit body when your tap root connection to the universal energy grid was tenuous. Whenever someone you cared about has disconnected his or her cord from you, or you from him or her, reflect on what you learned from your shared experiences. Remember, sometimes the separation is just for a time to allow yourselves to grow independently, especially if one of you had been in some way held back in personal growth as a result of the connection. It is not a good or bad thing. It just is what it is. If the break is permanent, you really have no choice but to accept it. Refusing to accept it only causes more angst within your spirit body and may unnecessarily taint your future life experiences.

A period when you are losing many connections is usually a transitory phase which may feel as though it has gone on for a very long time. Unfortunately, even though you have lost people in your human relationship matrix, new connections may not immediately present. During this time, you are in a period of transformation and are at a crossroads where you need to make a decision of whether you like who you are becoming. Once your human trinity has decided on the direction to take, the "right" type of connections you need for the next phase of your journey will manifest in your life. As these people enter your life and form new connections with you, it sometimes feels like coincidences. These connections, either good or bad, will propel you down the path you have selected. Depending on your life choice, this can be a great thing or a very bad thing.

PROXIMITY AND STRENGTHENING CONNECTIONS

Whenever you share space with someone, tendrils of umbilical cord connections reach out from your spirit body towards the spirit body of the other person. It reminds me a little of static electricity. If you were able to see it, it looks like a mini-bolt of lightning snaking out from your body when you get close to another person or object. While your spirit body is sending out tendrils of energy, so does theirs. When these tendrils of energy connect, your spirit body has just connected to theirs. If the tendrils did not connect, then your spirit bodies did not. In this early stage of connecting to others, if their energy is very different from yours or resonates differently, the ends of the tendrils of energetic umbilical cords reaching out from both of your spirit bodies literally repel each other. If the energy resonance is the same, they connect.

Interestingly enough, the polarity of your energy can sometimes affect this connection as well. If your energy flows in a different way than that of someone else, additional factors come into play. When polarity is different, your spirit body must make a conscious decision of whether or not to connect to another. At first, if the polarity of the other person is very different from that of most of the people you currently connect to, you might feel that the other is strange or you are not sure if you want to connect. Remember, polarity has nothing to do with whether the person is an honest, good person or not. It is just that his or her energy is different from your energy or the energy resonance that you are accustomed to interacting with. When the resonance differs, it causes their energy to push against your energy in a way that feels uncomfortable or unfamiliar.

Before connecting, your spirit body sends a message to your brain to assess the situation including information regarding the resonance of the other to analyze. It also informs your brain on its position on whether or not to connect. If your brain decides to connect, the connection forms. If not, then it makes the final decision on behalf of the human trinity and blocks the connection. However, there are times that the spirit body recoils so strongly to a potential connection, that it blocks the connection and tries to 'force' the brain to comply by activating the 'flight and fright' response. Many times, people with differing polarities are very slow to connect to the other. These are connections that once they form—even though they take a while—can be very strong and lasting. The flow of energy through mixed polarity cords tend to be more tentative at the beginning. Eventually, once mutual trust and respect are established, the flow of energy will improve. When energy comes through a shared cord, how you experience it differs depending on the energy sent. As energy comes through, you will feel tingly in the physical area around the affected chakra. If the energy comes through the heart chakra, a tingly feeling may be present around the heart area or you may have the sensation of your heart 'flipping'. When strong emotions filled with angst come through the heart chakra, recipients can feel like they are losing their breath, which can feel overwhelming.

There are times when you will sense the emotions of others who connect to you through the cord that has leached this energy into your spirit body. This can be experienced as a host of different emotions or feelings depending on the people around you and to whom you connect through your human relationship matrix. If you find yourself feeling down or blue, check whether the emotion is yours or whether you accidentally picked up the energy of another. If it is originating within your human trinity, you should be able to trace the reason for your sadness, feelings of inadequacy, or whatever other feeling you are having. If you cannot find the source of the sadness within you, start checking the cords. Initially, it might be difficult to determine whose energy is sad. You may need to reach out to those to whom you connect to find out how they are doing. Sometimes this will quickly reveal the source of the sadness. Then you can assess how their energy resonance feels when they send sadness energy through your shared connection so the next time they do it you know who is sending it.

You also have the ability to strengthen energetic umbilical cords with others. The most passive approach is to simply spend time together. As you spend time in the company of others, you are sending energy back and forth through the shared umbilical cord. This movement of energy is critical to the strengthening of this connection. Another way is to hold hands. As you hold hands with each other, you share energy through both the cord connection and the physical connection to the other person. When holding hands, your auras overlap at your hands and shares energy with the other through this medium as well. This also applies when you shake the hand of another. Have you ever experienced a time when you shook someone's hand but the moment he or she released your hand, you wanted to wipe it off? If this happens, it might simply be that his or her resonance is so different from yours that your spirit body wants to remove any traces of this temporary contact. When we hug each other, our auras overlap, contributing to improved connections. However, instead of a single point of connection, you are sharing energy through multiple points of contact. During a hug, your auras are overlapping over a large area. Depending on whether it is a full frontal hug or side hug, the degree of overlapping will differ; the volume of energy shared between the two huggers is much higher than simply holding another's hand.

For most people, connections form very easily and quickly, especially if you spend considerable time on a regular basis in the same space. Such people include coworkers or friends. However, there are times when we are forming or strengthening connections with people unconsciously as we sleep. If you are sleeping in a shared bed, you are strengthening the connection with the person with whom you are sleeping. You may even be creating new connections with them as you sleep. When a relationship has ended, but you still co-exist in the same physical space or share a common bed as you sleep, it can make it especially difficult to move on.

How effectively your spirit body creates new connections while you are asleep depends on how close to the other you sleep. If you like to snuggle or spoon as you sleep, you can forge new connections or strengthen existing connections organically. This reinforcement or creation of connections can lead to greater feelings of connectedness and even love. However, if you sleep on different sides of the bed, whether or not these connections get stronger depends on the size of the bed and the size of your spirit body aura. For example, if you sleep in a double bed, the spirit body auras of all occupants of the bed have a high likelihood of overlapping. This facilitates connections between the people in the shared bed. However, if you share a king-size bed, the likelihood of these connections becoming stronger or forging new ones drops dramatically. For some people, sleeping in a king-size bed causes stress on the existing connections, and from their spirit body's perspective it is as though both people are sleeping in separate beds. This can cause the connections with your partner to become weaker, more brittle, atrophy and break easily.

I am not advocating that everyone throw out their king-size beds. They are great for those nights when half of the couple is sick or is awake. It gives you the ability to distance yourself so that your inability to sleep or rest well does not affect your partner. However, if you want the organic strengthening of the love bonds as you sleep, you need to find ways to encourage this connection even though the bed is large. One way is to snuggle or spoon as you fall asleep. Then, for at least a portion of the night, your spirit body has the opportunity to perform maintenance on existing cords, reinforce them, or create new connections. If you do not like to snuggle and need your space in order to sleep, try to find a way for at least one part of your body to touch as you sleep, even if it is only your feet. This phenomenon also applies to homes and the physical spaces where you spend your time. If the house is large and you spend your time closeted away from the people who live with you, over time the strength of the cord connection can be eroded. Always try to find ways to spend time with the people you love to strengthen the love bonds between you. When we share time and space with others, we promote the growth and nourishment of cord connections by sharing energy through our cords as well as through our overlapping auras.

Chapter 5

ENERGY SOSS

Have you ever experienced times when the name or face of people connected to you through your human relationship matrix keeps popping into your mind? Maybe you felt an urge to call them or drop by their place unexpectedly. You may even experience an overwhelming need to reach them immediately and talk to them. This urge begins with an anxious feeling swelling up within your spirit body between your will and heart chakras. If you followed through on this urge and called them, but they did not answer, it can translate into a swirling of anxious energy that turns into a vortex of anxiety. When they did not answer, you may have dropped by their place or called on a friend or family member to stop in on your loved ones to reassure yourself that they were fine. Once a person who was on your mind was located, you may have discovered that something had happened—whether it was emotional or the person felt that he or she was in some sort of danger. These are examples of SOSs received through the umbilical cords.

Depending on your ability to sense energy within your body, some of you will be able to determine whether good news or bad news is coming. For those who read my first book, you would be aware that of all people sensitive to energy, the emotional intuitive type is most adept at sensing these types of vibrations. For them, the SOS messages tend to affect their emotions. If the person who is sending the energy is in trouble, the emotional intuitive feels unsettled or anxious within their human trinity. If the person to whom they connect is sending reassuring messages that all is well, they can sense this as well. Some can sense when a friend, lover, or family member needs them and determine who is sending the energetic SOS. They might even be able to sense SOS vibrations from people they don't know directly but are connected to through someone to whom they connect. They even sense happy emotions traveling to their cord from the network of those with whom they connect.

One of the gifts we have is the ability to send energy and messages through our umbilical cord connections with others. Like all energy we send through our shared cords, this energy pulses with the resonance of how the sender is feeling and often includes key details of what is happening in the other's life. When a mother senses something is wrong with her child through energy she received through the shared connection, it is referred to as a "mother's instinct." The benefit of developing this skill is great when you need to figure out if your child or loved one is safe but is unable to contact you electronically at the moment. Sometimes, this failure to communicate with you electronically is due to a technological issue rather than a situation where they are in some type of jeopardy. Some people have a keenly developed ability to send SOS messages through their cords with a minimum of effort whenever they even think about sending a message to someone.

There are many reasons that you may want to send out an SOS through your human relationship matrix. When sending these messages, the sender is often in a hyperactive stimulated state. It does not need to be due to a horrific situation, a crisis, or some type of physical emergency. It may simply be a message that something amazing just happened. Most SOS communications are simply urgent messages sent through the cord requesting physical contact or electronically facilitated contact to share information. The message may be the result of wanting to talk to a specific person whom you have not been able to reach through phone, e-mail or text. Sometimes, it is just because you have not heard from people in a while and you are wondering how they are doing. They can also be the result of missing someone, but you are not sure how they would respond because your last conversation was an argument; you want to reconcile but are afraid to contact them because you are not sure whether or not they are ready to talk.

It can be as simple as you have had a difficult day and need to talk about it to someone. You might even want to send out an SOS because you are lost and need assistance to get back to familiar territory. Then again, you may not be feeling well and want someone to help take care of you, but you feel bad asking someone for fear that he or she will say no. It could be that you are feeling lonely and want someone to reach out to you to be there without having to call and ask him or her to come over. You can even send them when you are scared or hurt or have a medical emergency but cannot get to a phone to call for help. Regardless of the reason why you send out an SOS, it is great practice to keep the energy moving and to strengthen our connections to others through this non-verbal communication network.

Even though you are not consciously aware of sending out an SOS, these messages are never "accidental" transmissions. SOS messages are the result of your spirit body and physical body both engaging, even for a brief moment, with a joint desire of wanting someone to connect with you—either in person or through an electronic communication tool. Your spirit body provides the energetic power and energy pulses, and your brain helps to compose the content of the message. Working together, they create a series of pulses of energy of varying lengths and resonances. Within these pulses of energy is important information that includes key aspects of who is sending the message, what is happening, and the action requested from the recipient after the message is read and interpreted.

SOSs are short pulses of energy in a stream sent with the specific purpose of having another do something to connect with you physically or do something to help them in some way. Every day, we send thousands of communications through our cords to those with whom we connect. However, this energy is passive, and the recipients usually do not feel that they must act on the energy received. It is the equivalent of chatting with someone about your day, but not really expecting him or her to do anything with the information other than listen. Every day, we are both the sender and recipient of massive amounts of energy and energy chatter through our cords using SOS communications. Energy chatter is similar to someone who tells their friends or family of every movement or thing they do during the day. Instead of electronically sharing this information through a social media application, they are sending you a moment by moment update through a shared cord connection. If you are sensitive to this energy, it can make your spirit body spin due to the volume of incoming energy. It is like having everyone to whom you connect all talking at the same time. It can be overwhelming. This is why it is so important to put filters in your cord to limit the information coming through. That way, you are in control of how much energy enters your spirit body. In your filter, consider adding your intent that the urgent and important information always reaches you. This filter limits the energy associated with their daily activities from passing through the shared cord, and keeps it on their side of the filter.

SOS TRANSMISSIONS

There are two types of SOS transmissions. These are *focused* and *general*. When you send out a focused SOS transmission, there is one person or a series of people whom you want to receive the message. The second is a general transmission, where you are sending out the message to whomever you can reach through the cord connection, regardless of how distantly connected they are to you. Of the two, the general transmission approach requires a lot more energy, since it needs to travel through more energy cord connections that are not directly connected to your spirit body.

Before you send out an SOS through your cords, there are a few things to consider. The first is your intended recipients. Depending on whether you want a person, a specific group of people, or as many people as possible, the energy you need to put into the energy pulse will differ. You need to decide whether it is a general SOS message where it does not matter who comes to your aid or responds—as long as someone does—or whether you want specific people to respond and reach out to you to help. When deciding, keep in mind that when the message is focused, you are dependent upon the ability of a specific person or person's to receive the message. If their ability to receive or interpret SOS messages is weak, there is a good chance that they will not act upon the SOS in the manner you expect, if they act at all. However, if you are sending a general SOS through the cords, you need to add as much energy as you can spare to help it travel to as many people as you can. When you release the energy, you need to decide whether to send it through some or all of your cord connections. Sometimes, a cord connection with someone who geographically lives the furthest from you can have a connection that is closest to you when you need the help. As you send the energy, make it clear that you are open to getting help from whoever can assist as long as they are safe and will not harm you in any way.

To determine the 'who', sometimes you need to consider what type of help you need. At times, it does not matter who helps you. For example, if your vehicle is on the side of the road and isn't working, and you need someone to see you and call for help, sending out a general SOS to reach as many people as possible might be more effective than sending one to someone who is far away and will take a while to reach you. In this situation, the SOS message sent through primary, secondary, and possibly tertiary connections asking for help triggers a motorist who drives past you to call an emergency line to send assistance your way.

Next, you need to determine what you are hoping will happen as a result of your sending the message. Do you want them to do something specific once they receive it? If you want them to come to your aid, then that is what you include in your message. If you want them to recognize you need help and send emergency workers to you, include that in your message. Then consider the purpose of the SOS. If you are sending a message to let primary connections know that you need their emotional support but cannot reach them through traditional methods, then include that in your message. An important thing to consider whenever sending messages is whether the recipient is capable of helping you in the way you need. If you are unsure whether a specific person can help, you may want to consider sending your SOS message to two or more people.

The urgency of the message is also an important consideration. If you need someone to act as soon as he as she is able and safe, and legal to respond, include that in your message. However, if you do not need the recipient to contact you immediately, but within a certain time, say an hour, then include that in your message. Sending a message without giving a time frame of when you need a response can result in people not responding to you in a timely manner. Then again, if you send everything as a "fire" requiring an immediate response, even if it is not critical, over time the recipients of your SOS messages will start ignoring the urgency of these transmissions. Even if you need them to respond quickly to an SOS that really is urgent, they might ignore it and reach out to you hours after the crisis has passed.

Be as specific as you can in the messages sent out in an SOS. The clearer the message, the more likely it is that recipients will understand what you need and act to help you. When you are sending out an SOS, you do not need to use specific words or specialized phrases. However, whatever you say needs to come from your spirit body, not just your head. Therefore, you need to focus the energy within you. If you are upset, worried, anxious, happy, elated, or whatever the emotion, draw on this energy and release some of it with your message. It adds a resonance to the energy you are sending that can make it easier for the recipient to know who is sending the SOS and your emotional state at the time you sent it. This energy can also help your message travel farther, faster. As you prepare to send the energetically charged SOS message, gather this energy into a ball within your spirit body and add the specific type of help you need. Then add who you need to act on this SOS. Add what you need help with and how quickly you need the help. Be specific.

If you want them to call you, stop by your house, text you, drive by your work, or whatever, decide exactly what you want them to do to help you. Add this intent to the ball of energy. Then focus your energy on the shared cord connection between you. As you release this energy through the cord, clearly state either aloud or under your breath exactly what is happening and what you need them to do in order to help you. Sometimes, the message is simply "XXXX, please call me. I haven't heard from you in a while, and I need to know that you are okay." It can be as direct as "XXXX, please come to my house. I'm hurt and cannot reach my phone." Your message might be that "XXXX, something amazing just happened, and I need you to check your messages *now*! I want to share my joy with you." SOS messages can be positive, neutral, or a request to act as quickly as it is safe and legal to do so.

The best time to send SOSs is when your spirit body is churning with energy. When your energy churns, it is building up energetic pressure within your spirit body that you are not grounding or sending back to the universe. This churning energy also activates the flight-or-fight response within your physical body. This contributes to the power of the SOS. If you do not attach very much energy to it, it is not going to go far and probably is not going to reach someone who can help you. As a result, sending an SOS is much easier to do when you are in the middle of some type of emotional situation where you have energy coursing through you. As you focus your intent on this energy and add specific details to your message, it creates a pulsating resonance on the energy to seek out the help you desire. This energy, once released, can be a ball of energy like a heat-seeking missile that does not stop until it finds a recipient who acknowledges the energy and acts on it. However, even though it is easier to send the energy when you are experiencing a strong energetic reaction to a situation, it is also a good idea to practice sending energy just to tell those to whom you connect that all is well. When you do this, they get a feel for your energy before a situation occurs where you are in need of their help.

RECEIVING AN SOS

We all have the ability to receive a SOS through our human relationship matrix. We can receive them from any of our primary connections, or through any of their shared connections with others. Although we can all receive these messages, it is easier for some people to sense these messages and correctly interpret the energy attached to them than it is for others. Regardless of your sensitivity to receiving and interpreting these messages, this ability is something that you can work on developing. Although you might never become an expert at it, just by noticing shifts in your energy and being able to determine who is sending the energy can help you reach out to someone who sent a distress call, even if you are not sure what is wrong.

When you receive an SOS energy transmission, it feels like a series of short, strong bursts of energy through the cord. Most of the time, this transmission generates a strong emotion within you. When your spirit body receives the package of energy, it immediately begins to try to figure out who sent it if it isn't yours. If you regularly monitor your connections, this step will go much more quickly. As your spirit body is processing, it sends a message to your brain stem with a download of the essence of the energy received. This is when it shares how the person is feeling, whether someone wants you to do something, and whether or not your spirit body thinks it is equipped to help. The brain stem forwards this message to the brain to process. At the same time, the central nervous system activates a response in your physical body that aligns with the intent of the message.

When many people receive an SOS, they feel it as a sudden shift in their energy and feel like someone has infused them with some type of emotion. Typically, they experience SOS messages as a surge of emotions or feelings such as panic, anxiety, fear, hopelessness, or a plea for help of some kind. However, if the energy transmission was weaker, the message received can be far more difficult to interpret. You might feel it in your spirit body as swirling energy that has a negative pull on it back toward the cord connection of the person sending the SOS. Your physical body might feel unsettled or off, but you may not be sure why. For others, the sender of the SOS will pop into their heads and they will feel the urge to call or text him or her. Some people are so effective in receiving messages, that when senders include an "image" of where they are, they can see it through their third eye.

For those who are psychic, receiving SOSs can be far more graphic. When they receive an SOS message, some receive a flash of the person sending the message, including what he or she looks like at that very moment. In the background, they can see the room or physical place where the SOS sender is at that moment as though they are standing in the same room.. They can see facial expressions, and they might even "hear" what the person is saying as the message is being transmitted. Within their spirit body, they can feel what the SOS sender is feeling at that moment. This flash sometimes lasts for only a few seconds but it is as though they are physically with the sender. This transmission of energy can last a few minutes depending on the power added to the SOS message and the ability of the receiver to sustain the connection. Regardless of how long it lasts, during the time it takes for the message to be received, the psychic has connected directly with the person. In some respects, this connection is similar to the way in which they connect to souls in the ethereal world.

The key is that when you are receiving these messages, the sender's name or face usually flashes in your mind's eye, or you have a brief thought that you should call them. Whenever you have a crossing thought of connecting with someone who is one of your primary cord connections, they are sending some type of energy through the cord that you are picking up. Depending on the situation, you might not be able to call them. For example, the person might be an ex-lover or companion and the physical relationship has ended. In those cases, you send help energy to help them, but you might want to consider the repercussions of contacting them before acting on the SOS. If connecting with them is going to cause more issues for either of you, it's probably best if you do not contact them directly. Instead, consider contacting someone who can connect with them to find out what kind of help they need and are in a position where they can help them out.

DETERMINING THE SOURCE OF AN SOS

When you receive energy, the first step is to determine whom it is coming from. To do this, you need to know what the energy feels like as it comes through the cords from different people. This is when it becomes very important that you consider how energy feels from different people—their resonance and energy signature. If you are not sure who is sending the SOS energy, send pulses of energy through each cord connection to determine who is struggling and needs some type of help. Although it is tempting to send a text message to everyone to whom you connect to figure this out, you might inadvertently send one when they are driving or operating some type of machinery. If they do not have a hands-free device or it is not permitted to talk on their phone when you are trying to connect, you could inadvertently get them into a more serious or dangerous position. When you are reaching out, you want to help and not contribute to a bad situation. Therefore, to confirm who needs your help, send a return pulse of energy to the sender asking them to call or text you when they can and it is safe and legal to do so.

However, there are times when the energy suddenly stops flowing through the shared cord. Even when you try to send energy to the person who sent the SOS, it bounces back. If you are sensitive to energy, it feels like your energy hit a wall before bouncing back to you with a small echo of energy. For many of you, it is more subtle and you feel the reverberation of the energy bouncing back. The energetic sensation is similar to the echo your body feels if you speak in an empty auditorium and your voice echoes back to you. This sometimes means that the person sending the SOS is reeling from some type of emotion so they are disconnecting slightly from their human trinity, or that they are unconscious. It might present as an overwhelming sense of panic or a knowing that something is seriously wrong. Some of you might even feel suddenly emotional and want to cry. This feeling does not necessarily mean that someone has died. All it means is that something is happening that is preventing your loved one from sending energy back to you. If the energy ceases abruptly and you have an immediate feeling of dread, followed by an energetic vacuum on the other side of the cord, that is not a good sign. When there is a complete void in the absence of the energy movement, it is usually due to the universe installing an automatic filter blocking communication of what was happening to the affected human trinity. It doesn't necessarily mean that they have died; it just means that they are being blocked from sharing energy with you. If someone has passed, the connection flips to the soul of the individual from their spirit body, creating a strange shift of energy or feeling within you. There is an odd numbness in your side of the shared cord, even though many emotions are coursing through your physical being. At that moment, some of you will have an intuitive sense that someone has just died.

PRACTICE, PRACTICE, PRACTICE

Your ability to receive SOSs and interpret the messages accurately takes time and practice. Regardless of how good someone is in sending out SOSs through the cord, if the receiver is struggling to pick it up or ignores the message, then the transmission of energy was not very successful. Conversely, if people struggle to send out SOS messages or cannot clarify the intent of their SOS distress calls, this can make it extremely difficult for the receivers to determine who sent it or what is wrong. It makes it impossible for the receivers to figure out what the senders need from them.

This is where practicing sending out SOS messages helps both senders and receivers become better at sending effective energy transmissions through the umbilical cords. It is helpful if you practice ahead of time by sending energy to each other to get a feel for what their SOS energy feels like. When you first begin to practice, start by sending an SOS message to one person. Before doing this, let the person know that you are going to practice sending a message. This gives him or her the opportunity to practice receiving the energy and focus on how your energy feels. After sending the message, ask the person what he or she received from you. Be sure to give your partners a little time to figure it out. Usually this will take a few minutes.

In the beginning when people practice sending and receiving messages, the receivers may not be even remotely correct on what the senders thought they sent. When they do not get the message exactly right, focus on what they did get. At times, the message received includes a passing thought of the sender that made its way into the transmission. It is important that you do not place blame on anyone for garbling the message. Sometimes, the underlying issue is that senders were not clear or did not focus their energy. At times, the problem is that receivers are just not very sensitive to receiving SOS energy and receive only a very high-level sense of the intent of the message. It may be that when you are practicing, one or both of you are distracted. Conversely, it may be that you are not practicing when you can leverage your spirit body's swirling energy to help focus your message to send it through the cord with more power.

When you are first learning how to focus your energy into an SOS transmission, it helps to use the energy swirling within you from real situations where something invoked your emotions. It just easier and faster to access the energy needed for an SOS when there is excess or build-up of energy within the spirit body. Then again, you can always draw the energy from the universal energy grid or from your environment to send the message. The benefit of practicing when there are real emotions coursing through your spirit body, your recipients of the SOS message can sense how your energy actually feels when you are upset, worried, scared, nervous, etc. Otherwise, you will need to try to manufacture this energetic resonance into your SOS transmission, which can be more challenging to do.

I must admit that I routinely send out SOS messages as a way to give my friends and loved ones a chance to sense my energy at different times. I tend to test them out on a regular basis when I know they are at home. I often start with small things. If I am wondering where people are, I send a SOS through the cord asking for them to call or text me when it's safe and legal to do so. There are times I have lost someone's e-mail address, so I ask him or her to e-mail me. I even send them out if I have not heard from a friend or loved one in a few days asking them to send me a text, call me, or pop in to see me. When they receive it and respond, I let them know I sent a message. Then we talk about how I felt when I sent it and what they received. This gives both of us a chance to practice these skills and to learn how much energy is needed when sending a message before the recipient can pick up the vibration. This also helps both of you to figure out how much energy and information is required for different degrees of urgency. When it is something big and you have practiced the normal daily angsts, then recipients will know the energy vibration is much stronger and that what is happening is more significant than before. This sometimes is what indicates to others that the SOS transmission has a resonance of urgency.

I know that I could easily send a text message or call the people to whom I send SOS messages. However, I like to practice using our cord connections to send messages. Practicing sending this energy and having others sense your messages are definitely helpful if something happens and we do not have the ability to call or text for help. Like exercising any muscle, you should practice sending and receiving SOSs through your energetic umbilical cord connections before you really need to. Think of it as a test of your emergency human relationship matrix broadcasting abilities. When you become good at sending and receiving messages, it gives you the ability to determine if someone to whom you connect needs you.

If you find that you are struggling to sense the energy from others within your spirit body due to SOS messages, you might want to consider installing a filter within your cord to detect SOS messages. I tend to put energetic filters in every shared cord I have with others. The SOS filter serves as an early warning detector to let you know if someone to whom you connect needs you. Refer to my book *Taking Back Your Joy of Living* to learn how to create and install filters in these shared cords. When installing an SOS filter, be sure calibrate to how the person's energy feels on a "normal" day. I tend to calibrate it to how they are generally feeling. If they are going through a difficult time, I reset their filter to neutralize this energy. This makes it easier for me to sense whenever their energy is more positive or negative than usual. It is the shifts in their energy's magnetism that inform you whether they are having a good or bad day.

Using your ability to send SOS transmissions through your cords also helps you build stronger connections with those with whom you share a primary cord connection. As you send and receive messages, if there is a problem with the transmission on either end, it gives both of you the opportunity to figure out what is happening. If there are leakages of energy in the cord, which can happen if either of you send negative energy at the other through the cord when angry, this gives you a chance to rebuild the connection. Damage to the cord may suggest that you need to renegotiate the relationship and rebuild the friendship or possibly create a new cord connection. However, if you never tested your abilities to send SOS transmissions to them, you will never know there was work to do to repair the relationship before it reaches a crisis point where a single interaction could fracture the connection forever.

Chapter 6

DNA, YOUR ENERGETIC CALLING CARD

As human trinities, we have a physical body and a spirit body that our soul infuses with the essence of our authentic self. Due to the superimposing of your spirit body and the effectiveness of the two-way communication network within you, every molecule of your body resonates as you. As you know, we shed dead cells from our physical body daily while forming new cells. Essentially, every day, our physical being has the opportunity to recreate itself one cell at a time just as our spirit body rebuilds itself with refreshed energy from the universe. With this continual rebirth of cells within our physical being, it means that even in identical twins, there can be small genetic differences due to mutations that occur during cellular division.

Within each cell you shed into your environment is a small packet that connects itself to your human trinity. This is your DNA, or deoxyribonucleic acid, which contains your genetic code. This material is referred to as our genes and is the building block of our physical being. Our genes contain a host of information that affects the final physical product of our human being and is the essence of who we are in a physical sense. Through it, your physical being emerges from mere cells into your human form. Your DNA dictates your height, the color of your eyes, and hair and skin color, as well as a host of other factors that contribute to the uniqueness of your physical being. It also contains predispositions to diseases or conditions we will get or are susceptible to developing depending on a variety of factors. Sometimes these predispositions activate due to environmental factors, or from things we do, eat, or drink.

Although at first glance one would think that our DNA only resonates with our human trinity while it is connected to our physical form, this is not always the case. I suspect that even in ancient times, our ancestors knew that there was something special about our physical being. In fact, in some ancient cultures, they not only mummified their kings or leaders, but they also spent time with the mummified form. It is believed that some ancient cultures consulted their mummified ancestors in their attempts to access divine knowledge or obtain direction on what they needed to do next. Some cultures are believed to have paraded with the mummy, or practiced their most sacred or important rituals in the presence of former leaders' mummies. By doing so, they believed that they could connect with the person who passed.

At first glance, these practices might seem to be a strange in modern times. However, you may be doing this yourself and not even be aware of it. Although we may not parade with the remains of our loved ones or practice sacred rituals in front of them in the modern world, we at times still consult the "mummies" or remains of our loved ones for divine help. Let me explain. Whenever you visit the grave of deceased loved ones, you are putting yourself in the presence of their mummified physical being. Many of you talk to deceased loved ones at their grave, telling them about the important events in your life. If you have the ashes of a loved one who was cremated, you might display them in a prominent place or keep the ashes close to you in your most private or sacred place. At times, you might even pick up the urn or talk to your loved ones' ashes as though they were there. Regardless of whether your loved ones were buried or cremated, some of you might even ask them to call in a favor, or ask the angels to intercede on your behalf to improve the circumstances in your life or remove roadblocks from your life path.

This instinct to communicate with the souls of our loved ones while we are close to their physical remains is not new. I think that on an instinctual basis we "know" that we can connect to others when we are close to their physical form, or the remains of it, even though their soul has passed on to the other side. Although you may hear different rationales for this, I believe that part of this instinctual knowledge lies within our genetic code, as well as in the way our human trinity functions. Since your spirit body superimposes on your physical being, it senses what is happening within the body and has the ability connect with your physical body's DNA, and shares this with your soul.

Not only does DNA contain information on your genetic makeup, it also has the same energetic resonance and signature as both your physical and spirit bodies. In essence, your DNA is your energetic calling card left behind by your physical being. Regardless of where you leave DNA, your spirit body has the ability to reconnect to it. Therefore, it is a powerful connection back to your human trinity. It is also a powerful connection to those you share similar DNA with, including parents, brothers, sisters, or other relatives. Some people are very sensitive and can sense whether people share DNA with them just by touching them or being near them. You have probably heard of stories where people have "known" that a child was theirs just by holding them. You might also have met people who "knew" that a child was not theirs, and they were later proved to be right. It gets interesting when someone meets a "long-lost" family member. Some feel the immediate connection, while others feel nothing. Your DNA is the energy signature of your physical body. This energetic signature infuses all of the energy you release. Even if you are an identical twin, there is a small difference deep in your genetic code indicating that you are in fact unique.

TROJAN HORSE ATTACKS

As the energetic calling card of your human trinity, your DNA has both the energetic signature and resonance of your spirit body and the genetic signature of your physical body. Some people are so sensitive to this energy that it can profoundly affect their spirit body when they encounter this discarded energy power pack belonging to another. Using your DNA, some people have the ability to connect to you in many different ways. For some of you, connecting to others using the DNA they have left behind is relatively easy. This is due to the fact that your discarded DNA has the same polarity and resonance as your human trinity. Essentially, it is magnetized to you. If someone adds their energy or negative intent to it, and the energy is sent directly back to the source human trinity, it can be repatriated as though it is your own energy. The danger with this is that it makes you susceptible to people who use your DNA and energy trace to send negative energy or intent your way.

Whenever someone sends energy your way, your spirit body is aware of the incoming energy. If it does not resonate with your human trinity, your spirit body senses this. Your spirit body can choose to block it, deflect the negative energy, or send it back to the sender. It is similar to your immune system in your physical body. If a bacteria or virus enters your body, if your physical body notices it, it will immediately launch an immune response to destroy the invader. You spirit body is the same. To defend against invading energy, it needs to realize the energy resonance and signature do not belong. If someone uses your DNA and energy resonance to cloak their negative invading energy, it can pass through your defenses and repatriate with your spirit body as though they are simply returning your energy. This is because your spirit body recognizes the DNA's energy signature as part of your human trinity. In essence, they have just used your DNA as a Trojan horse, preventing your human trinity from immediately detecting the invading energy. At times, a person skilled with using energy can use your genetic material to attempt to cast negative intent or spells your way. They are counting on your DNA and energy resonance to cloak the energy they put on it to pass through your shields unimpeded.

You may be wondering whether I am going to tell you exactly how to add energy to another's DNA to use it as a Trojan horse. I will not. When you know how to do it, in a moment of weakness, it can be very tempting to use their energy against them and send negativity using a Trojan horse. However, whenever you do this, it might affect their ability to practice their free will within their lives. Most of you reading this book would not want to do this anyway, since it is against one of the universal rules that we all enjoy. Specifically, the right to use our free will to make decisions that affects the path or direction we take in life.

Whenever someone tries to control another, it affects the other's ability to be his or her authentic self. Over time, the controlled person may become angry or feel like a prisoner, and the relationship transforms into a toxic relationship that can have terrible outcomes for both. Although Trojan horse attacks can be effective in harming the entire human trinity of another, there are karmic ramifications for using them.

SENSING THE ENERGY ON ANOTHER'S DNA

Although there are karmic impacts of using another's DNA in a Trojan horse attack, you can access the energy in another's DNA to sense where they are and how they are feeling. It interesting thing about DNA is that it contains the resonance of the person the moment they shed it. It is like a snapshot of their essence at that moment of time, just as though you took a picture of the person. If they were in a negative place energetically, it will resonate with negativity. To sense this energy, it is best if you are not physically touching the object with the DNA on it. This prevents you from contaminating it with your energy and skewing the energetic signature.

To begin, find a comfortable place to sit at a table where you can place your feet on the floor. Then place the DNA sample or object with the DNA on it on the table. After you sit down, make sure that your body is in a comfortable position. Now you are ready to begin. With the DNA source in front of you on the table, close your eyes and hold out your hands toward the sample. Clear your mind of your thoughts about the individual. Now consider how the energy from the DNA is making you feel. Can you sense the resonance? Was the person angry, upset, happy, peaceful, or experiencing some other emotion when he or she shed the DNA? How strong is the person's will energy? Is he or she trying to manifest something in life?

Consider the charka energy types. Can you sense trace amounts of chakra energy on the object? If one of their chakras was moving energy very quickly, or was overtaking the human trinity, sometimes the DNA sample almost has an aura to it aligning with the chakra energy. As you step through these questions, you may get flashes through your third eye that show you what your subjects have been wishing to happen in their life. What does their energy say about how they feel about you? This is when you send a small burst of your energy toward the object to determine how this energy bounces back to you. If a person passionately dislikes you, if you are sensitive to energy, you might be able to pick this up. Connecting to the DNA of other people can have unexpected results. It can be as simple as touching a pen of another and their energy residue and DNA on the pen indicated that they were afraid of you because you communicate with spirits. Upon reflection, you may realize that the last time you saw them with the pen, they were playing with it as you spoke about the spirit who had communicated with you recently.

If people have passed, you can use their DNA or something with their DNA on it to try connecting with them. Again, starting with the DNA in front of you, send out a message to them that you would like to talk with them. As you hold out your hands toward the object, try to connect with their energy signature. If you are successful, you will sense their presence or smell strange odors that are not usually in the space. For example, you might smell lavender, cigar smoke, cigarette smoke, perfume, or even the smell of medicine. At that point, start asking questions of the soul and wait to see what information they send back to you. Depending on your abilities and the ability of the soul, they can use a variety of ways to communicate with you. One way is through flashes of images in your third eye. Another is using sensations within your physical being. Regardless of how they communicate, it is not always easy to decipher their messages. Then again, there are times you want to ask questions that they really do not want to answer. Instead, they will talk about what interests them. When the soul steps away or you are ready to end the connection, simply state that you are ending the connection and thank them for coming through before moving away from the DNA source.

SHARING DNA WITH ANOTHER

We share our DNA information with others in many ways. At first glance, you might think that you do not share your DNA with others.

However, you probably do in a variety of ways. Whenever you kiss, epithelial cells from within your mouth can transfer to the person you kissed. If you lick an envelope to seal it, you just gave the receiver some of your DNA. If you write a letter, you leave traces of your DNA on the paper. When you sneeze or cough, you spew traces of your genetic material into your environment. You also leave DNA left behind in beds, clothes, furniture or any other physical object others have touched or been near. If you consider all of the ways you share DNA, the list is quite long.

At other times, we give away some of this genetic material. If you donate blood, you are giving the gift of life to someone who desperately needs it to survive. However, it contains massive levels of your DNA, your energetic resonance and your life force of your physical body. If you are not careful when donating blood, the receivers of it may have the ability to connect with your human trinity. Some may find that the recipients of the blood can directly connect with you until their body ultimately destroys the blood and their body replaces it with blood their body has created. This can become worrisome. Do not worry; you do not need to stop donating blood. Instead, if you donate blood, you really need to pull back your energy signature from the blood and replace it with a different resonance that blocks others who receive your blood from connecting with you. I will talk about how to do this later in this chapter.

Whenever you leave your DNA behind or willingly share it with others, others can use it to connect directly to you. This is why some practitioners use hair or some form of DNA when they are casting spells on others. Your DNA has your signature on it, and they are attempting to tap into this resonance in their attempt to bypass your shields and lodge an attack against your human trinity. To avoid the misuse of your DNA for such attacks, you need to pull back your energy signature and resonance from your DNA.

To do this, you need to start by intentionally asking the universe to pull back your energy. Another way is to use your intent to remove or change your energy resonance on the DNA you leave behind. Whichever way you choose, first consider what is being left behind— can someone easily access it, and how much DNA is connected to it? If the DNA left behind is in bodily fluids, and are immediately absorbed by a porous surface containing the DNA of others, it is generally harder for someone to access it and use it in any way. The energy attached to it quickly dissipates and is harder to isolate from other DNA energy left behind in a space. However, if the DNA is collecting in a shared bed that you leave, they can connect to you while in that bed. If your DNA is in the form of hair or blood, it is much easier to use it to connect to you regardless of the location of the samples.

Regardless of how they get your DNA, the reality is that we all shed it every day, and we leave a trail of our genetic material behind. Therefore, you should consider pulling back your energy from it. You might want to consider doing this a few times a day. To do this, you simply ask your energy associated with your discarded genetic material to return to the energy grid for recycling. If you are concerned that someone might use it against you, then you want to change the polarity of it. This is something that you may want to do at the end, at the beginning, or in the middle of each day. It tends to work best if you do this as part of your meditations. Specifically, when you are in a meditative state, connecting with the divine, ask that the polarity on any genetic material that you left behind or donated have a "discarded" resonance added to it. Also add the intent that your human trinity will repel all energy connected to others trying to repatriate your energy using your DNA with their intent hidden within it as though it were a Trojan horse.

Then, although the DNA still identifies with your physical body, any type of spell or intent placed on it will be repelled by your spirit body, which will recognize that the energy attached to it is slightly different from your trinity's energy. You could even change the polarity of it so that whenever you release any genetic material from your physical body, the polarity of the energy on it immediately changes so your spirit body will repel it. Energetically, it would be like trying to push together the two positive ends of a magnet. They will push away from each other. As such, it is critical that you change your energy signature on the DNA you shed to ensure it resonates differently from that of your human trinity.

When you change the polarity on discarded or donated DNA, your spirit body pushes away any intent or energy that another places on genetic material or sends your way using its resonance. If you donate blood, just before the technician or nurse inserts the needle to take some of your blood, ask the universe and use your intent to change the polarity of the blood. To do this, as the blood enters the needle and goes into the collection bag, visualize that the metal of the needle immediately changes the polarity of the blood taken and removes your energy signature from it. In its place, a resonance consistent with water used to sustain life infuses it. Using your intent, state that the sole purpose of this blood is to help replace the blood another lost, save or prolong the life of others and that the DNA in the blood loses all ability to reconnect with you, the donor.

An easy way people can connect to you is using a bed that you have slept in or shared with another. The reason for this is because it is a single piece of furniture that you spend many hours in daily. As such, it becomes infused with both your DNA and energy resonance. If you have ended a relationship, regardless of whether or not you keep the bed, you need to remove your energy resonance from any genetic material of yours that was caught up in the mattress. Likewise, if you travel and sleep in hotel beds, you are leaving your genetic material behind, as did everyone else who slept in the bed. This includes hair, skin cells, bodily fluids, or any other type of cell that has DNA captured within it. I have to admit that when I go to a hotel, I often try to connect to the energy of others to find out if they had a good sleep in the bed. I have learned that I prefer rooms with two double beds to give me a choice of which bed to sleep in, depending on the bed's resonance. Depending on my resonance of the day, and many other factors, I will select the bed that best accommodates my energetic needs or wants of the night. The interesting thing about hotel beds is that they have the energy from so many different people who slept in the beds infused into them, that it is more difficult to use this energy to connect to any particular individual.

Regardless, the most effective way to remove your energy from a bed after sleeping in it or spending time on it is to start by being in the same physical space as the bed. However, you can also do this from a distance and use an object to represent the bed. Before beginning, make sure that everything you need to do this is readily available—such as holy water, sage, or incense. I prefer holy water. If you like to hold some type of talisman in your hand as you move energy, have it close by when you do this or hold it as you usually would when dispelling energy.

Before you begin, you may want to start with a meditative state or do something that raises your energy to make it more concentrated and focused. To do this well, you first need to achieve the state where you can feel the energy coursing through your body and hear it move. It would be like a person who has high blood pressure lying down and being able to hear blood push through his or her veins. You do not need to be angry or upset; you just need to be pulling in energy at a fast rate from the universal energy grid. In a later chapter, I talk about the ways energy feels and sounds when it moves that are typical of different spirit body types.

Once you have established a strong movement of energy through yourself, face the bed or the object representing the bed. You can be at either side or at the foot of the bed. However, if the foot of the bed is higher than the mattress, you probably should do this from the side of the bed. All sheets and covers should be off the bed. Relax your shoulders, and place your feet shoulder width apart or in a stance that feels comfortable. Next, raise your dominant hand toward the bed at waist to chest height, depending on what feels the most comfortable for you. Then tell the energy resonance, DNA and discarded biological materials that are yours that you have divorced yourself from them. From this moment onward, they do not have the ability to reconnect to you in any way. If someone tries to use them to connect, their polarity immediately changes and their energy is repelled from you. Then sprinkle holy water onto the bed to cleanse it of your DNA energy signature. Although this can help disconnect you from your DNA that permeated the bed, your residual energy and energy signature can persist long after your DNA signature has been removed.

Chapter 7

CONNECTING TO THE UNIVERSE AND THE ETHEREAL WORLD

Our spirit body has the ability to attract energy from the cosmos—from the divine, from others, or from the souls of people who have passed. As we resonate with either positive or negative energy, we are like a tree in a lighting storm. We become the lightning rods and attract similar energy to what we are putting out, back into our lives. When you are consciously managing your energy and sending out the most positive resonance you can, you are increasing the likelihood that good things will come into your life. This ability also permits you to pull strong bursts of energy into your spirit body when it is needed.

Consider lightning and a tree. I have always been awestruck and afraid of lightning storms. There was something about how the air felt electrified under the large tree in front of my home I grew up in that unsettled me. There was also something about the power of lightning strikes that frightened me. The thought of how quickly the lightning could cut a tree, or cause a fire terrified me. I knew that trees are more likely to be struck by lighting and that you should never stand under a tree during a storm. I also knew that the distribution of positive and negative energy within the tree shifts. However, on several occasions, as lightening lit up the sky around a tree, I thought I seen a flash of energy like a mini-lightning bolt or a finger of energy towards the sky from the tree. I am not certain if I was seeing something from a psychic perspective or if it was a real physical thing. Regardless, it seemed to me as though the tree were attracting the highly charged energy in the sky.

Whenever I seen this flash of light from a tree during a storm, it reminded me of how static electricity shoots from my finger at times with a small zap of light and a small shock of energy as I touch someone or something. I believe that we also send out tendrils of energy toward the divine and attract energy to our spirit. The difference is that when we are sending out positive energy to the universe, we are attracting like energy into our lives. This comparison made me realize that like a tree, our spirit body can act like a lightning rod when massive amounts of energy come directly at our spirit bodies. Considering the tree struck by lightning … it quickly sends the charge into the ground and into the air around it. By moving the excess energy quickly, it limits the physical damage to itself. The same phenomenon applies to our spirit body. When we get struck with massive levels of energy, it needs to go somewhere to avoid significant damage within our human trinity. The more effective we are in moving energy back to the universal energy grid and out of our spirit body if we sustain a direct energy strike, the better our chance of limiting the damage to ourselves.

One way to ground excess energy building up in our spirit body is through our energetic taproot. Every spirit body has a taproot from the moment our human trinity forms. Using our taproot, we connect to the universal energy grid, the source of all life. Without it, our planet would be barren, and souls in human form would not be able to exist. A fundamental purpose of our taproot is to supply our spirit body with refreshed energy from the universal energy grid. It also allows us to pull energy from Mother Earth to manifest good things in our lives. Another function of our taproot is to serve as our lightning rod to divert excess energy that strikes our spirit body or builds up within it as we experience highly charged life events and return it to the universal energy grid. Whenever we use our energy, the expended energy turns into waste energy in the form of residual energy. Using meditative techniques and our taproot, we can release the residual energy that has built up within our spirit body back to the universal energy grid. Through our spirit body, we also have the ability to draw in energy from Earth elements, depending on our spirit body type, to ground ourselves.

CONNECTING TO THE SPIRIT OF A LOVED ONE

After the trinity expires, souls tend to remain close to the people in their human relationship matrix for approximately fourteen days. During this time, the souls of people who previously belonged to that human relationship matrix who have passed gather close to the soul that has recently died in the physical sense. However, if someone is particularly bad, there is a chance that angels will pick him or her up the moment the human trinity expires and escorts the soul to the other side. However, this is very rare. Usually, the soul retains its universal right of free choice. The universe steps in only if there is a risk that the soul will continue causing harm to the spirits of others from the other side.

After approximately fourteen days, the souls pass through the white light portal into the vestibule or foyer of heaven. Here the spirit loses all contact with people on the Earth plane until it has finished the purification process. What happens during this process is subject to speculation. Whenever I have asked the angels, their response has always been that the universe tailors this experience to the individuals, what they have done, and what they need to work through as part of their cleansing and life debriefing. They did explain that while in this state, they process what they learned during their current life's journey, finish any life lessons they missed if they committed suicide, and see how their life choices, decisions, and actions affected and continue to affect others.

Once a soul finishes the initial purification process, it joins the divine with the angels, is sent for punishment, or goes to the waiting room to await reincarnation into a new human trinity to continue on its journey. Typically, souls that have finished their journeys go to the divine if they have reached a level of purity to become a minor angel. "Hell" is the destination for those souls that the universe decides requires some form of serious punishment before it is determined whether they can have another chance to change and grow. For others, the souls of the people who died go to the waiting room where they hang out waiting for the remaining members of their soul group to rejoin them. This gives them the opportunity to see the ramifications of their actions in the human form that continue to plague those whom they hurt. Others gather and start planning when they would like to return to life in the human form. While in the waiting room, they can communicate with loved ones on Earth either directly or indirectly through psychics or mediums and share their messages of love, hope or validation to those who are still in the physical plane.

Interestingly, if a soul is in the waiting room and tries to exert too much control over someone who is still living, it can place him or her in serious trouble with the divine. At times, they become involved because someone in the physical plane has asked them to do so. However, we all have the ability to practice our free will. If a deceased loved one tries to control someone who is still living in a human trinity form, regardless if it is on their own behalf or in the interest of another, they are violating the universal right of the person to make his or her own decisions. If they are using strong influencing techniques or pretending to be an angel, a group of angels charged with escorting souls violating the universal rules to a zone where they lose all ability to communicate with those who are living will meet with them. If deceased loved ones communicate with you, remember, they are still imperfect. Even though they may tell you to do something, it is your choice to do what you believe is right.

Here in the physical plane, if we violate the rules of our societies, punishment may result. It is no different in the spiritual world. If souls violate the right of free will of those here on Earth, the angels lock them in a holding area where they have no ability to use their energy to influence anyone. Think of it as solitary confinement. When the angels place them in this energetic chasm, they cannot see what is happening in the earthly realm either. This period of isolation can be for a short duration or until the last person whom they tried to control is no longer living in the physical realm. Upon release from this energetic lockdown, they can choose to return to Earth or they can stay in the esoteric realm. However, a condition of their release from this holding area is that they follow the rules.

COMMUNICATING WITH SPIRITS

The ability to communicate with spirits is a tremendous gift. However, a greater gift is to be able to turn off their noise and focus on living your life and fulfilling your life's mission. If you have the ability to communicate with spirits, your ability to block their energy can make the difference between feeling sane or possessed. As for myself, I have been able to communicate with angels as well as with the spirits of the deceased from a very young age. At times, the communications felt overwhelming and it felt as though all the spirits were battling for my attention. It was like being in a room with hordes of people with everyone speaking about different things all at the same time and trying to speak louder than each other. The noise got so loud and overwhelming that it was hard to hear myself think.

Even worse, some would pose as spirit guides to try to get me to do their bidding. I knew something was not right, so I asked the good angels for help to quiet the voices. I also asked the angels to teach me how to tell the difference between my guides and the musings or wishes of spirits of those who have passed. The first thing they taught me was that I had the ability to close this communication channel temporarily without worrying that I would lose this ability for life. When I was open to receiving the messages, they could come through. At times, it was as simple as my telling a spirit that the person they wanted to chat with was not available and it would be better if the three of us could talk together. That way, I could share their messages and if their recipient had questions, they would have the opportunity to answer them. From time to time, particularly strong spirits continue to pop in to chat. They do like to play games though. If you can hear them, you may find yourself responding to them calling out your name even when you were trying to ignore them.

It is much more difficult to tune them out when you are in a large group of people. I still find that there can be an overwhelming crush of spirits coming at me if I go to a mall during peak shopping seasons. Whenever there are masses of people, the spirits desperately trying to communicate with their loved ones can become overwhelming, especially when you are not in the right environment to share the messages received. There are folks who would not be terribly happy if a stranger stopped them to tell them that "Uncle Ed" says hi and shares personal family messages.

Spirit energies can be active at any time during the day. However, I find that they are the most active around 3 a.m. Regardless of where you live or the actual time, I find that they are the loudest around the time that my body is in its liver detoxification phase. I have also found that spirits can communicate with you in different ways. Their souls literally connect with you on an energy plane and talk to your spirit body. One of the ways they communicate is through images, like flash cards. Some can talk to you if your spirit body can hear them. Others share information telepathically. The effectiveness of this communication depends on the strength of energy of the spirit and your abilities to connect. As a result, the communication can be as clear as it would be if you were standing next to the person you are talking with, or difficult to understand as though you are talking to someone over a bad telephone connection.

At times, the spirits wait until their loved ones are asleep to talk to them. You may have experienced this. They come in a dreamlike state, and it feels "real" as though you are physically spending some time with them. When they are communicating with you, some of you will find yourself reminding them that they are dead. Most of them know that they have passed. Remember, it takes a lot of energy for spirits to connect to those who are not psychic or have limited ability. If you spend too much time talking about them being dead, you may not have the opportunity to talk to them about what is in your heart. They are visiting because the love connection or umbilical cord connection to you is still active. For some of you, this is the only way that they can communicate with you directly to let you know that they are all right.

When spirits communicate with me, I find that they act in ways that are eerily similar to how they were in life. If loved ones were controlling in life, or always thought they knew best, this trait does not leave them. When they visit, they tend to continue giving their mandates and expect us to follow them. Sometimes, they try to force you to do or act in a way that you do not wish to. Remember, just because they have connected, there is no need for you to do their bidding. Accept their messages and information as you would if they were living. You still have control over your own human trinity, and whether you are going to act on what they talk to you about or ask of you is up to you.

The souls of those who have died have the ability to communicate with their loved ones or others even when the recipients of their messages do not want to talk to them. I have found that they can become quite creative in trying to communicate with you in these circumstances. Some will use electronics and mess with your computer, type messages when you are trying to text someone, or even change the channel on your television. Others will make the lights flicker or cause your phone to ring a single time. Of course, there is never anyone on the other end. Then there are those who take a strong hands-on approach and make sure that you know they are there. These spirits touch you or poke you to get your attention. If you can hear them, they call out your name. When you respond, they know you heard them. I had one say, "Gotcha," when I responded. I must admit, it was a little annoying.

My first experience with this was when I refused to communicate with the soul of someone who had passed. If I get a message from a spirit, I prefer to immediately share what the individual said with the intended recipient. In this situation, I was not even sure how I would be able to pass on the messages. After many attempts to communicate with me, the spirit got my attention by stepping through my human trinity. I could taste the medicine the spirit took prior to death on my tongue as it stepped through me. It was awful. It was a very uncomfortable feeling, and I could feel my entire body turn ice-cold. At the same time, I could hear my spirit body yelling at me to move away from the spirit. As quickly as the spirit stepped into my human trinity, it stepped right back out. Of course, I had also moved to the side to get away from this invasion. In case you are wondering, this experience taught me the importance of shielding myself so such an invasion could not happen again. Once was more than enough.

When spirits step through you like that, it is not a possession. Rather, they are being obnoxious and showing you that if you do not want to talk with them, they can make it very uncomfortable for you. If you experience this, remind the spirits that they are infringing on your human trinity's free will and that you refuse to let them do it again. Place a shield around your spirit body that blocks any spirit from stepping through you. If a spirit steps through your trinity, you can tell them to go away. Usually, this is enough. If it isn't, ask the angels to help you. If spirits do this to you to get your attention, or play with your technology, whether or not you decide to listen to what they have to say is up to you. If they step through me, there isn't anything that they can say that I want to hear or pass on. If you choose to listen to what they have to say, once they have finished sharing, you can choose to accept the information or to discount it. When you listen to what they wanted to share, they tend to be far more likely to step away.

Not all spirits are strong enough to step through your human trinity in order to get your attention when you are refusing to communicate with them. However, there are other ways they can and do communicate with you. Some will connect to other spirits who communicate with your spirit guide. I had one relative who blew cigarette smoke into my face. She did it for approximately an hour every day for nearly a month. When I asked what she was trying to say, she was silent. I knew that she was trying to tell me that someone had lung cancer and was dying from the use of the cigarette smoke. However, she was unable to tell me who it was. Finally, fed up with the smell of cigarette smoke blown into my face daily, I asked her to talk to my guide so my guide could tell me what she wanted to share. Through my guide, she was very successful in sharing the entire message she had for me.

For spirits who struggle to communicate with your guide or want to talk to you directly, they can essentially get "their people" to talk to "your people." This is when they get their spirit guide from their most current lifetime to talk to yours. Then your spirit guide lets you know that the soul is trying to communicate with you and shares the essence of his or her message. At that point, it is up to you to decide whether you want the soul to connect directly with you. However, if your spirit guide is suggesting that you should talk to the individual, you probably should listen to what the soul wants to share. Sometimes, it is what you need to get closure. The ability to accept the person's words and move past the death or hurt from the person's actions can be freeing for your human trinity.

CONNECTING TO SOULS BY USING PHYSICAL OBJECTS

For centuries, people have tried connecting to the spirits of their loved ones using a variety of methods. At times people who want to connect to spirits from the other side use devices such as a "talking table," a communication table, or other device so that the spirits can move a physical object to communicate. The danger with this practice is when you are actually successful in connecting with a soul. Personally, I find communication tables or other devices can be very effective in releasing the energies of those whom the angels have locked away for the protection of human trinities. Many of the spirits that are accidentally released using these tools are from one of the seven levels of hell, and they use the guise of communicating with the people using the device as a way to escape. The reason for this is that the combined energy of the people around a talking board collectively asks the universe to release a spirit to communicate. The danger is that if two or more people join in intent, believing something will happen or manifest, it might actually come to fruition. This applies to any situation when two or more people are focusing their energy, asking the universe to allow them to communicate with a spirit. They may end up receiving more than they intended.

It has been my experience that when a talking board or table is used, the people you are communicating with are not your loved ones. They most likely are nasty spirits posing as your loved ones to gain your trust. Not only do you connect to a spirit you did not mean to, if the spirit was bound for humankind's protection, it can now return to Earth and can haunt one or more of the people who facilitated its release. The spirit might haunt the house where the ritual took place, or it can travel to haunt another. This can create a horrific experience for the people who are sharing space with this evil entity.

A safer way to try connecting with spirits of those who have passed if you are not particularly psychic is to visit a medium. Before visiting one, always let your loved ones know that you plan to visit a medium in order to talk with them. Remember, the spirits of our loved ones are busy on the other side visiting with those whom they love or hanging out with people in their soul group who are on the other side with them. This advance warning that you hope to communicate with them makes it more likely that they will step forward when the opportunity presents itself. When they do, some of them are so loud that the medium has to share their messages first before moving to the next soul. I personally found that if you let them know that you are going to a medium that is very good at communicating with them, they tend to show up early for the meeting. Some will be with you starting the day before the reading. If you have a pet, you might find that the pet starts acting strangely. For example, dogs tend to notice the energy of souls when they are in your space. If you are in the same space as both your dog and the spirit, your dog will keep looking at the spirit and back at you. It is as though the dog is trying to let you know that you have a visitor.

There are many ways to connect to souls of your deceased loved ones. You can try connecting by wearing a ring or a piece of jewelry that once belonged to a loved one. Another way is through a piece of their DNA such as a hair clipping. Other ways includes clothing or furniture that they loved. What all of these objects have in common is that their loved ones have left traces of their DNA on these articles as well as their soul's resonance, which makes it easier in some ways to reconnect with them. Some people even light candles on the anniversary of the death of their loved ones. As they do this, many feel closer to their loved ones. At times, they might even feel that their loved ones are with them, visiting with them as well.

Some people reading this can connect and communicate with the spirits of those who have passed simply by holding an object, picture, or something that belonged to the person. Literally, they are using trace amounts of residual energy clinging to the object, DNA, or a picture of the individual to open a communication channel with the person who passed.

NEAR-DEATH EXPERIENCES

Some people have near-death experiences when their physical body shuts down, and they see heaven or a celestial place. Once they are there, an angel tells them they need to go back and continue living their lives. You may be wondering how you can "die," see heaven, and then come back into the physical body. As I explained previously, if your soul leaves your sona, then the trinity disintegrates and both your physical and spirit bodies die. If this is true, then how can one have a near-death experience? What is really happening when people have these experiences? This is something that I asked of the angels. I wanted to understand how it happens from a spiritual and energetic perspective.

What I learned I found fascinating. The angels told me that part of the answer is attributable to a core function of our spirit body. Although it superimposes on the physical body, it can also act separately and distinctly from our physical body and our soul. As I explained in Chapter 1, our spirit body forms one of our multiple consciousness through which we experience life. It has the ability to reach to the divine, the esoteric realm and the Akashic records to access guidance, comfort, information and knowledge. The spirit body of a psychic, medium, clairvoyant, etcetera, are highly developed in its ability to reach out to the spirits of people who have died and to communicate with them. Some can physically "hear" them talking; for others it is telepathic hearing, or seeing symbols with predefined images.

Near-death experiences typically happen when something traumatic is happening to the physical body or there is a looming threat of physical death. When their physical body starts shutting down, prematurely or not, or if their physical body is placed in a state of suspended animation through medical means, their spirit body can take flight. Although it connects to the human trinity through the sona, it tries to remove itself from experiencing what the physical body is going through. Remember, there is two-way communication between the physical and spirit bodies. However, instead of the spirit body stepping to the side of the physical body to oversee what is happening, it travels through a white light portal while still maintaining the very thin ethereal connection back to the sona.

The white light portal is what souls use to travel between the earthly plane and heaven when they are not part of a human trinity. Although this portal is not for them to use, their spirit body feels the life force dropping in the physical state, feels the force on the sona, and may even "know" the soul is at a predetermined "checkout point," and it goes to the light. Before birth, each of us selected "checkout points" where our soul must choose whether to continue in the journey, or to abort the mission and leave the sona. When we reach these checkout points, something will happen in your life. It can be a near-miss where you may or may not even have been aware that you bypassed a checkout point. Other times, a dramatic event occurs such as a serious accident, illness or situation where you are aware that your life was in jeopardy.

They remember this experience once they reawaken because they never lost their connection to their human trinity for the entire trip to the ethereal world. As I mentioned in a prior chapter, the spirit body communicates its experiences with the physical body, and vice versa. When the spirit body travels through this portal, the physical body might be in a coma-like state. For some people, the physical body may not show signs of life as vital signs may drop below detectible levels. Others enter a deep, trance like state. In this state, their lack of responsiveness in the physical being can last from a few seconds to hours. It will last as long as their spirit body is in the passage to the other side.

As they travel through the portal, they see some of the things they have done and how they affected others or themselves. This process gives them a sense of their life "flashing before their eyes." However, this experience is not to the same degree as one's soul experiences. At least, that is what the angels have told me. I am taking their word on this. For some people, this traveling experience is something their guide arranged with the angels. Their story may have a profound effect on those around them and helps others in some meaningful way. Essentially, this experience was to be a life-changing event to remind them of the life mission that their soul promised to do prior to birth. At the end of the portal, the souls of those who love them, or connect to them through the human relationship matrix that have passed, greet their spirit body. Essentially, their spirit body has entered the "foyer" of the afterlife that some call heaven. It is very bright with the light from the souls and angels and is quite beautiful. Energetically, this space has a very peaceful, loving, and calming energy. There are also angels guarding this entrance. Although you can visit it using your spirit body, you cannot stay. It is the angels' job to ensure that only souls remain in this place.

Remember, this is the place souls pass through after their sona tears open, releasing their spirit, and they lose their connection to their human trinity. As they go through the portal, their spirit body stays behind with the physical body. For some, their souls are in a state of shock. Here the newly deceased receives a blast of unconditional love and acceptance. At that moment, the soul needs comforting that it has left behind those it loved. They have a moment of clarity and realize how their actions affected others in life, and that they cannot change the events they set in motion. These angels are not there to judge the newly passed souls; their role is to direct them to where they need to go next. The guardians of the other side are also there. These angels escort the newly departed to the purification zone. Their job is to help souls move to the appropriate zone where they will enter to debrief on their life experiences. This is where the newly departed also witness first-hand how their choices and decisions are continuing to affect those who remain on Earth with the living.

Only your soul can pass through this space to move on to the next step of its journey deep into the ethereal plane; your spirit body cannot. Think of this space as a busy airport with souls rushing around in different directions. Anyone can enter the airport, but there are parts of it you cannot enter if you do not have a valid plane ticket to fly to a designated place at a specific time and date. The same premise applies to your spirit body. It can enter the foyer and spend time there with deceased loved ones and the angels present, but it cannot stay, and the spirit body is told it is not its time and that it needs to go back.

When the angels send the spirit body back, they also send a jolt of energy through the spirit body to reanimate the physical body and into the sona. Essentially, they zap the soul with divine energy to get back to work if its energy is waning. This energetic zap restores energy movement through the physical body via the sona. Depending on how long the spirit body was in the ethereal plane, there might be physical implications from the tenuous connection that has placed additional stress on the sona, nearly causing it to open and release the soul. Then, as the spirit body returns to its homeostatic state within the human trinity and is no longer reaching into the ethereal world, it communicates with the physical body what it just experienced. Once these people awaken, they realize that they have just had an amazing experience.

You might be wondering whether the person actually died and rose from the dead. Even though the person had a real experience visiting the vestibule of heaven and met angels and loved ones, he or she did not actually die. Technically, you die in this physical world when the sona opens and the soul returns to the ethereal world. The spirit body returns to the universal energy grid for recycling, while the physical body eventually turns to dust. Until the sona opens, there is a chance the person will recover. The human trinity is still alive. Whenever someone has a near-death experience, this exerts tremendous pressure on the sona. At any time during the journey, if the spirit body travels too far, it can tear itself from the human trinity. When it does this, it will tear open the sona, thereby releasing the soul. Once the soul is released, the human trinity disintegrates. With this in mind, the fact that the person visited the ethereal plane using their spirit body and had this experience is quite amazing. Not everyone can say that they visited with the angels and those who passed before them in such an intimate way and lived to tell others about their experience.

Chapter 8

SPIRIT BODY TYPES

There are four important functions of your spirit body that are independent of which spirit body type you have. It is the body through which your soul expresses its authentic self. Your spirit body is infused by your soul with the essence of who you are or are striving to become as part of your soul's journey. Together they are your "spirit" within your human form. Another role of your spirit body is to draw energy from the world around you and from the universal energy grid and infuse your human trinity with energy. Just as your physical body has the ability to take energy from the food and water you drink to sustain your physical life, your spirit body also needs energy to survive. Its third role is to facilitate connections to the divine, to the spirit world, and to other human trinities. In the physical world, this ability allows us to form strong bonds with others that sustain us emotionally or energetically when we are going through difficult life situations if we choose to allow them to help. It also allows us to connect to the divine as we navigate through our life's experiences for guidance, help, inspiration, and even comfort.

Through your spirit body, you can experience life in all degrees of energy whether it is positive or negative. Your spirit body is also part of the early warning system that alerts you when others throw negative energy at it, warning you of potential energy strikes that can injure your human trinity. When you are in tune with your spirit body, you will find that it is always on alert and is attuned to the energy coming at it or building in the cosmos toward you. When you can hear or sense this energy, it puts you in a better position to ward off an attack or promote healing within your spirit body if it has been hurt.

As your physical body has gifts, so does your spirit body. Within each spirit body type are gifts and opportunities for improvement as we enact our free will within our human trinity. As I did with my first book, I pondered how much information I should share with you regarding spirit bodies. Inherent to every spirit body type are positive elements, opportunities for improvement, and negative elements. I know that for my personal development, I needed to look at my spirit body from an objective perspective in order to determine what I needed to work on. If you are like I am, if I do not share both the positive and more challenging aspects associated with the differing spirit body types, it may negatively affect your own personal growth.

As you read this section of the book, keep in mind that the intent of the examples and characteristics outlined by energy type is to give you a better understanding of the more common strengths and weaknesses of each energy type. This in no way means that if you have a specific spirit body type, you possess all of the characteristics depicted. You may not. We are all individuals and are all unique. You may have had the same spirit body type in your past lives and learned how to manage different challenges it may possess—or you may have mastered a potential weakness in your spirit body during your current lifetime.

When you examine yourself through an objective lens, remember that no one is perfect; we all have challenges to overcome, and we all have positive energy characteristics and a spark of divine greatness in us. It's important to remember that depending on the situation you are in, the characteristics of the spirit body type you have can be a benefit or a liability. Furthermore, by giving us both good characteristics and those that are a challenge to overcome, the universe in its divine wisdom offers us the ability to practice free will through our spirit bodies. I hope that by understanding the potential strengths and challenges of our own spirit bodies and those of others, we can all embrace our similarities while fostering an environment that is accepting, loving, and understanding of each other's uniqueness and gifts.

There are four primary spirit body types: fire, earth, water, and air. In the water spirit category is a fifth spirit body type that has elements from each of the other body types, called a chameleon. If you were to compare the spirit body types to the Chinese elements, the chameleon falls under the metal element and air falls under the wood element. People of each spirit body type have the ability to draw in energy from their environment in a form that aligns with their spirit body type. Air energies draw in energy from the air around them, water from water, fire from fire elements, and earth from the earth beneath them. Chameleons have the ability to draw in energy from any of the four elements. However, their preferred source of energy is usually water, which is why they are in the water spirit category. Although our spirit bodies have many gifts, at any time a gift of your spirit body can become a liability to overcome.

To understand how our spirit bodies move energy, we should start with the spirit body types, the environmental sources of energy they draw, and some basic characteristics. Remember, there is some natural overlap in some characteristics between differing spirit body types. It is sometimes the result of you consciously learning skills to overcome a "weakness" in your spirit body. This only adds to the uniqueness of your spirit body. However, if you are presenting some characteristics inherent to another spirit body type, it makes it a little confusing to determine the spirit body type.

This phenomenon is similar to our physical forms. Even though one has a pear-shaped body, not every person with a pear shape has the identical curves, measurements, and form as another pear-shaped person. Individual variances contribute to the uniqueness of our physical forms. Your spirit body is the same. There are many individual variances. Due to the life experiences of the individual, or skills acquired in this lifetime, we sometimes present "learned" behaviors rather than our authentic spirit body type. Think of it as "plastic surgery" on your spirit body. The underlying spirit body has not changed, but you have done things to it in order to help you better fit in or hide sensitivity. Our spirit bodies allow us to morph ourselves, to hide or reveal different aspects of ourselves if we need to in order to survive.

Depending on your spirit body density, you might display some of the characteristics in a more vibrant or muted way. If you have already worked on your energy, you may discover that you have overcome some of the less positive aspects of your spirit body and they are well under control. Remember, by facing our challenges or potential weaknesses, we have the best opportunity for success in growing spiritually and energetically. Although our spirit bodies are amazing in their ability to help us process energy and make sense of our world, the gifts they possess can become personal obstacles in our lives if we allow them to stand in the way of our soul's growth. The challenge is to draw from our strengths and work on our weaknesses to grow into the "best" versions ourselves. Although I will outline some of the high-level characteristics of the spirit body types, for more details on spirit body characteristics, and some of their challenges, refer to my book *Taking Back Your Joy of Living*.

EARTH

Those with earth energy spirits tend to be deep, calm, and reassuring to others. Others view them as dependable and even-tempered, and their demeanor encourages confidences. Those interacting with them tend to describe them as neutral and grounded. However, they can seem to be a little gruff or blunt at times, especially when they do not put up with anyone's nonsense. Their natural grounding ability and their solidity of energy can make it difficult for them to change paths or directions in life. This characteristic sometimes leads others to think they are stubborn, immovable, or closed off to "new" ideas. Some misinterpret reactions from earth energy people on a topic or situation. If people share upsetting news and the earth energy person shows little emotion while processing the information, others may interpret it as ignoring them or not listening to them. At times, others may perceive the earth energy person to be lacking in tolerance, which may not be true. Unfortunately, when earth energy people are upset, worried, or troubled, they pull back into themselves so strongly that they can seem to be cold or distant.

Interestingly though, when they talk, they tend to give away their spirit body type. Remember, the physical body and spirit body superimpose on each other, and both bodies are involved in processing information. When they are learning something unfamiliar, the words they use to explain their understanding of the material has some type of physical reference to it. They tend to say things such as "That feels right," "I'm not feeling comfortable with that," "I can get behind that," "I can support that," "I'm not feeling it," "It just doesn't sit well with me," "That doesn't feel right," or "I'm just not getting how that can work." It is as though they are examining the information through their spirit body and analyzing each part before they can accept it to be true. Many ask numerous questions when the information does not align with their beliefs.

At times, it seems as though they take longer to learn information than the other spirit body types do. This in part is due to the depth of detail they learn about a topic. If they are passionate about a topic, the depth of their knowledge can be vast. In this group, once they learn something, it is as though they never forget it. When something changes or does not "fit" in with what they believe to be true, it is as though they are mentally "cutting out" the old information and replacing this "hole" with the new. As they do this, they ask many questions to make sure it aligns with the rest of the body of knowledge they possess on the topic. Typically, they follow a more linear process when analyzing this new information.

Generally, they identify their own limitations and sometimes those of others very quickly. Sometimes this quick self-assessment can limit their potential for success when they do not take a chance and push past their comfort zone. When they get into a life path they find comfortable, it takes the equivalent of an energetic earthquake to get them moving in a different direction. They sometimes forget that life is not "all or nothing." Although they can be very creative thinkers and innovators, they may let go of a dream too soon if they do not see immediate success from it or if it is interfering with what they believe are their responsibilities in life. However, instead of letting go of their dream, their life goal might be to work on achieving their dream in their downtime. Although it is more work, while they are working to pay their bills, they can be using their dreams as a creative outlet. It will help them reach past the confinements of their human trinity and dare to dream of a different reality. For those with an earth spirit, this can be quite difficult to do at first. However, like anything, once they get moving in that direction, they can be difficult to stop. It is like pushing a large stone sitting at the top of a hill. At first, it is difficult to get it to move, but once you get it moving and it starts rolling down the hill, it is extremely hard to get in front of it to stop it without it crushing you beneath it.

As a group, they tend to be peacemakers who subjugate their own needs for others if they feel the others are more deserving of getting their needs met. This subjugation might lead them to start believing that their wants or needs are not as important. Another characteristic that seems prevalent with this spirit body type is that it demands that everything they do or learn has a meaningful purpose. Although this tendency allows them to get a job done in a focused manner, they can forget that sometimes the purpose is simply to have a little fun in a safe way. Instead of focusing on reaching some goal or on getting something done, it is sometimes just as important to enjoy the journey taken to get there.

As a whole, they tend to be very slow to get angry. This is the result of their stuffing residual energy residue so far down into their spirit body that it can change their resonance and magnetism. This characteristic affects their ability to achieve the calm, peaceful existence that they seek. At times, because they have stuffed down so much, over such a long time, when they blow, it is like a volcano spewing ash into the air, and lava flows all around them, making it harder to approach them. Since they tend to have very long memories, when they get angry, they spew energy related to hurts that have happened decades before that they never indicated even bothered them.

FIRE

It is hard to miss people with a fire spirit body unless their life experiences have subdued their inner fire. People with a fire energy spirit body tend to be passionate people who have their emotions stirred easily and might blast the unsuspecting person with a wave of red-hot energy without even meaning to do so. When motivated to do something, they are fast movers and can be hard to stop when they put a plan into motion. It is almost as though they are on a life quest to prove something to themselves, to others around them, or to both. When they are learning something or are communicating with others about something they are unfamiliar with, they tend to use words such as "I get how that works," "I just don't see that," "I can't picture it," "What I see is XXXX," "I'm just not following that," or "I just don't get it." Their words tend to have a visual or physical action aspect to them. It is as though to "see it," they also need to feel it moving within them to some degree.

They tend to be perfectionists who set impossibly high expectations for themselves and are overcritical of themselves if they do not measure up to these demanding standards. Unfortunately, when they feel as though they are "failing," they can sometimes take out their frustrations on those closest to them. Although they work hard, they tend to play even harder. To de-stress, they tend to put considerable pressure on their physical being to achieve feats that they personally find to be challenging. Although fire energies tend to have more intense personalities and sometimes appear to be strong energetically, they are also very sensitive. If you say the wrong thing or accidentally push a trigger point, they can have an over-the-top reaction to how you just hurt them. Remember, they move energy fast. When you push one of their buttons, they tend to react before they process all of the information, including your intent behind what you said or did.

Those with a fire spirit body type are the quickest of all spirit bodies at moving energy. Their speed of transmission is partly due to how their spirit body's energy supercharges after someone stokes their passions or anger. Fire energy people draw in energy quickly from their environment and cord connections, mixing it with their fire energy to create a tornado of fire energy. This fast-moving fire whirl can sometimes be difficult for them to contain before it bursts out of their human trinity and strikes out at those in the immediate vicinity, or sends the energy flaming through cord connections. For some, this translates into issues in managing the ferocity of their energy that others may perceive as anger management issues. Generally, they are passionate, intense, and mesmerizing when they are present in a situation. However, their intensity can scare away others with whom they are trying to build relationships. Although they tend to push others away with the strength of their energy, they often want to fit in and feel like they belong.

With their ability to move energy quickly, those with a fire spirit body can make quick judgments of others based on very little information. At times, they base their assessment on the resonance of another when it is not the same as theirs. Unfortunately, they may misinterpret this difference as another being less than truthful with them when this is not the case. This misinterpretation can cause tremendous angst for both the fire energy person and the person who they think is not being truthful.

Their ability to move energy quickly also means that sometimes they react so fast in a situation where emotions are involved that they say or do things to hurt others, only to learn later that their actions were not justified for the situation. Unfortunately, it may mean that they are reacting based on limited information, but they think they have the "right" solution. The result is that others may think that the fire energy person overreacts to something that in reality is really not an issue. However, in that moment of time, their spirit body has already linked this event to another situation where they had to act quickly to avoid some type of catastrophe. While the fire energy person is in this mind-set, if someone offers an opposing view of how to resolve an issue that the fire energy has already decided on how to resolve, the fire energy sometimes blasts the person's ideas without really hearing them. At times, fire energy people are so focused on "why" the other's idea is flawed that they come across as condescending or arrogant, even though that was not their intent. Sometimes, with this inner drive and feeling that they must "solve" the problem, they may ignore the input of others which may be perceived as devaluing another even though that was not their intent.

AIR

For those with an air spirit body, the sky is the limit. As a result, they tend to seek out roles in life where they are in an authority position, such as a teacher, an "expert" in some area, or a leader of some kind, including coaching roles. Many airs under the age of thirty tend be viewed as changeable or as not having a clear vision of where they want to be or what they want to do. As they become older, they tend to appear more grounded. I suspect that this is partially due to the energy residue that they drag around within their spirit bodies. For air energies, any amount of residual energy will feel "heavier" in their spirit body than in any other spirit body type. As they are one of the most adaptable spirit body types, some view them as changing just for the sake of changing. However, they are changing only because they believe that they must to keep growing or to adapt to an environment they find themselves in.

When presented with new information, they tend to process the information through their heads first and analyze everything. Of all spirit body types, they tend to be "in their own heads" the most. When they are learning new information and are heavily processing it, they tend to use words that reveal they are analyzing information and actively comparing it to other information. They typically follow a random, abstract pattern of thought as they work through the information. Their phrases might include "If this is true … then how can XXXX be true?" "I think I am missing something," "I need to think this over," "I cannot see how that "fits" with XXXX," "But XXXX said this … so how can YYYY be right?" Rather than removing the old information, they attempt to make the new information "fit" into their body of knowledge. This tendency may result in them immediately dismissing new information if it conflicts with something they believe to be true.

Some are always trying to best themselves as though life is a competition of how fast they can plow through their life experiences. They often feel driven to learn "everything" on a topic that interests them to become "the best" in that subject area. This really is a great gift, but it can sometimes get in the way of their achieving their life goals if they begin obsessing about something. At times, they can fall victim to an inflated sense of their own abilities, which can get them into trouble. Interestingly, when someone suggests that maybe someone else is "better" at something, or disagrees with their self-assessment of their abilities, air spirits will use words such as "I feel deflated," "they popped my bubble," or something else that indicates that they have lost air energy. When this happens, they can spin and start doubting everything they believe to be true about their abilities. It is important that they remind themselves that even though they do know a lot on a topic, it is okay if someone knows a little more. It really does not devalue their knowledge or contributions.

Although not as emotional as a person with a water spirit body, there are times they can run through many different emotions within a minute. When they are powerfully upset, they can mimic a person with water energy when their spirit body contracts and they cry more easily. Remember, air is a lighter form of water. However, these spells are relatively short-lived. Generally, they tend to be quite effective in getting their point across. When they are passionate about something, they can motivate others with their words. As a group, then tend to be very vocal. They have the ability to be the spokesperson for others. However, when they are the spokesperson for others, some attribute what they are saying as personal feelings rather than to those of the group. Sometimes, they are so vocal that they speak before filtering the words coming out of their mouth. Without meaning to, they can energetically hurt others.

Those with an air spirit body tend to have good communicating skills and are effective in informing others of what they think. The downside is that sometimes it is better that others do not know exactly what they are thinking. Sometimes when they are being vocal or someone stirs their passions, they may say things that they cannot easily take back or rectify. In their words, you can feel the heat of their anger or frustrations if they do not pull back their energy. Their excellent analytical skills mean that sometimes they overanalyze situations or the actions of others. When doing this, they sometimes project what they would do or what their own actions mean in a similar situation onto others, which might not be valid. As an expressive group of people, they are excellent communicators using their physical body.

Of all the spirit body types, this one is the most likely to learn skills that they view as "preferable" in order to achieve their life's goals.

If they view grounding their energy around others to appear calm or stoic as a positive characteristic, they will seek out the skills to ground energy within themselves and sometimes in others. This is actually a very good thing. Since those with an air spirit body can mimic a balloon floating through space with little or no grounding, the ability to pull down their energy is a great way to overcome one of the major challenges inherent to their spirit body type. Those with this spirit body type are so adaptable, they need to remind themselves that it is okay being exactly who they are rather than trying to conform to the expectations of others. As an air, they can compress and draw deeply within themselves. However, their greatest gift is the ability to be the rush of fresh air stirring others into action.

WATER

Of all the spirit body types, this group is the most diverse, with hidden depths to their energetic abilities. Unfortunately, they tend cry more easily than the other spirit body types, which they find incredibly frustrating. Even when they are raging with anger, they have tears in their eyes or running down their face. To stop this, some stuff down their energy so hard that they appear cold or immovable when angry. This leads others to think that they are either too emotional or too serious, depending on the situation. Like the earth spirit body type, they have the ability to stuff down their emotion or hurt for an incredibly long time, even years. Unfortunately, if they do, it eventually breaks out in a storm of tears or a tsunami of emotion that can last for many days.

Overall, they are very trusting and tend to project their intentions on others. However, if you betray them, you might lose their trust permanently. As people pleasers, they tend to subjugate their own needs in their attempts to make others happy, comfortable, or content. However, when hurt, they can shut down and walk away if a relationship is no longer "worth the effort." This cocooning of their energy is a natural protective gift. However, if they do this too often, they could find that they have cut themselves off from living or anyone who cares about them leading to profound feelings of isolation or loneliness.

They tend to process new information through both their head and gut simultaneously. When learning something new, they need to know "why" something is right or logical before it "sticks" in their brain. If they cannot rationalize the information, they can forget the material very quickly. When they are learning new material, the words they tend to use are varied. It depends on the density of their spirit body and the type of information taught. Examples are, "I can see why … "; "I don't understand how … "; "Why do we do … that way?"; "I'm just not getting how that can work"; "This isn't feeling right"; "That feels right"; "I got that, but why … "; "I'm lost"; "You lost me at XXXX"; or "It just isn't sticking." People with water energy flip between linear and abstract thoughts when processing information. The more stirred up their energy becomes, the more abstract the connections between cause and effect can become. Unfortunately, this sometimes results in them reaching a conclusion that seems "random" to others but makes perfect sense to them.

People tend to gravitate to water energy people as a calming influence when they are upset. They know that spending time with them and talking to them about the problem can help them feel better. As people pleasers, water energy people are willing to be there for them and comfort them as they work through their pain. However, if you have water energy and you forget to release this energy back into the grid, you might end up carrying around another's sadness or obsessing over their hurts for days. Those with water energy spirits sometimes obsess about a hurt over and over again until no one really wants to hear about it as they are trying to sort out their feelings. There are times when they are trying to make decisions that affect others that their energy can have a churning vibe that makes them appear moody.

Your desire to share your knowledge inspires you to teach others, and you tend to seek out formal teacher/trainer roles or more informal roles like sports coach or mentor. The driving force behind these choices is that you tend to get a thrill out of helping someone learn something new but tend to be self-deprecating in the breadth of your knowledge or abilities. Teaching is not about being viewed as the "best," or as having "knowledge power" over others; it is about how much you helped someone else. When teaching, you can become very passionate about the topics you are sharing with others. Sometimes, others may find that you are a little too passionate due to the volume of energy you release as you teach. This passion can be a little overwhelming to others.

You have the ability to motivate people to make positive changes in their lives, but you must believe in it first. Those with a water spirit body tend to cut new paths in life. Unfortunately, sometimes it is the wrong one. It you go down the wrong path, it can be very difficult to turn back or make a different path. Sometimes, part of the issue is that you may not want to admit to yourself the amount of time you wasted doing something that did not get you where you wanted to be. This leads into the water spirit body's tendency to be a perfectionist. The standards they set for themselves can be unachievable. However, they would never expect another to achieve the impossibly high standard. They can be overly critical of themselves and send many negative words about their own abilities to the universe. They can really become their own worst enemies.

At any moment, the water energy can change from calming and serene, to stormy and swirling. The ability to change the energy flow is an excellent gift. However, if they are continually in flux, it can affect their ability to ground their own energy, leading others to think that they are moody. Since they do not always see themselves as moody, if someone tells them they are moody, it can really upset them. Interestingly, those with water spirit bodies have the ability to identify the root cause of a problem or situation. Often without meaning to, they use their energy to clear away all of the distracting information on a topic, issue, conflict, or event until they reveal the underlying issue. However, by digging so deeply, they sometimes learn information that they would rather have not known. This can create a sense of unease or angst over what they should do with the information.

Chameleon

Although I classify a chameleon as a water spirit body, they inherently act as any of the energy types and routinely switch through the energy types in moments. When considering this spirit body type against the elements, a chameleon would be metal. At any time, they can manifest challenges of any of the other spirit bodies, and the energetic load to manage this spirit body type is massive. Even if they do not consciously ground their energy, they can mimic that of the earth energy spirit and then immediately flip to mimic a fire energy spirit. The reason for this is they have three distinct layers of water energy.

The outside layer is like a watery mist with the density of heavy fog or steam. The next layer has the density from water to liquid honey, while the third is very thick like solid creamed honey, or can be as dense as those who have earth spirit bodies. At any time, the density of any of the layers can fluctuate while the thickness of the layers changes in predominance depending on what is happening in the life of the chameleon at that time. In turn, the central layer can become very thin, while the outer layer becomes thicker. If this is the case, then the chameleon is in a situation where they are dealing with many energetic attacks and are trying to protect it by sending more energy to the outer edges, which can burn off rather than allow the energy to strike their inner core.

Chameleons are extreme people pleasers to the point that they may jeopardize their own happiness, success, or money to help others. They can sometimes be overgenerous to those they love. At times, a chameleon can seem very moody or excitable. Conversely, they can remove themselves emotionally from a discussion and become observers even though they are actively participating in a conversation. The passions of a chameleon can be stirred easily if they are not careful. When they are passionate about something, it is difficult not to join in their passion. At other times, they are like the air spirits and seem to be bouncing around, trying to figure out where they fit. Although some water spirits can have energy characteristics similar to earth energy spirits, how they process energy is dramatically different.

When chameleons get angry, they can access fire energy, resulting in a volcanic eruption of energy that burns everyone in its path. Although all spirit body types can and do get angry, their anger gathers within the core of their spirit body and swirls, and as they are blowing up, they are pulling energy from the universe through both their taproot and at least one chakra. When they spin, it takes a tremendous amount of energy to stop it. Another difference is they are usually uncomfortable with the power of their anger, which they tend to keep under tight control. Chameleons tend to worry about getting angry because they can energetically burn everyone in their path, much like fire energy spirits. When they do this, they create a whirl of energy that is fire, steam, and water. If someone causes the chameleon to release this extreme energy, the relationship with the person who made him or her angry is usually over. Both the chameleon and the target of the person's anger tend to step away from the relationship. However, after the chameleon releases a firestorm, they are usually filled with regret and cry.

Chameleons are unique in the way that their spirit body is continually fluctuating between densities at any given time. The unique thing about chameleons is that others struggle to figure out what type of spirit body they have because they are so changeable. There are times they act like earth, air, fire, or water. Even in similar situations, they may not act in the way you expect based on prior interactions. This makes them very hard to read unless they allow someone in and let them see or know how they think, what is important to them, or why they do things or act in different ways, even though on the surface the situation looks identical.

DETERMINING SOMEONE'S "TYPE"

If you are a light worker or a practitioner of some type, you might be interested in the spirit body type of someone when treating their physical body or spirit to promote healing. It is extremely important that you have correctly identified your own spirit body type. This is going to become the baseline spirit body type you will use to determine the how the spirit body of another differs from yours. You will also need to be able to feel or hear your energy move as well as energy movement in others. This is where it can become very difficult. Even though you are able to feel or hear your spirit body energy, you may not be able to sense the energy of others. Therefore, your ability to read the spirit body type of another is strongly dependent on your intuitive ability, energetic sensitivity to others, and ability to feel the spirit body energy of others. It is easier to do if you have a good working knowledge of how the differing spirit body types move energy. Conversely, you can use the spirit body characteristics to eliminate some of the spirit body types that they cannot be.

Chameleons have a small advantage in sensing the spirit body type of others, since they have a combination of the four types of spirit body within them. Essentially, to determine the spirit body type of another, chameleons test the resonance of another's spirit body against the different energy layers within them. To be able to do this, chameleons need to be aware of energy differences within their spirit body and be in a balanced, calm state. Some are so good at this it is as though they have an innate "knowing" of the spirit body type of another. If another's spirit body energy resonates similarly to the chameleon's inner core, the other has an earth spirit body. If the other's energy resonates similarly to their middle layer, then the person has a water spirit body. When the other's energy resonates similarly to their outer layer, they are air. However, if the other resonates with a similar frequency to that of chameleons when they are angry, they know the other probably has a fire spirit body. Of course, whenever the chameleon senses resonations similar to their multilayer resonance, they know they are in the presence of another chameleon.

Chapter 9

"Hearing" Your Energy Move

Within your spirit body, you have a highly sophisticated energy system that includes chakras and meridians. Through your energy system, energy moves within your spirit body, into your physical body and can move in any direction at will. It is a highly adaptable, fluid entity animating your physical body. If your spirit body is expressive, your physical body is also expressive and vice versa. Your spirit body has a resonance and magnetism that charge your human trinity with energy while acting like a well-developed energetic antenna that automatically draws like energy to it. It also has the ability to draw in energy from your environment, depending on its body type, as well as pull in energy from the universe. Before your birth, you selected your spirit body type. Regardless of the spirit body type you have, it came prewired to draw energy from the universal energy grid as well as from the environment through the elemental energy sources of fire, water, air, or earth. Your spirit body has the ability to release energy into the environment and to the universe, allowing you to manifest your wants, desires, or even fears into your life. It is one of the greatest universal gifts.

It has the ability to release residual energy stuck within in from life experiences. We all carry around different degrees of residual energy in the form of baggage within our spirit bodies. Some of us are better than others at letting this old energy go to prevent past hurts from damaging our futures. Regardless of your spirit body type, once it releases the energy residue holding you back and sends it back to the universe, this energy is engulfed by the universal energy grid and reabsorbed for recycling. One of the best ways to passively remove this residual energy is to continually draw in new energy through your spirit body through meditation, yoga, or even taking time outside to breathe in fresh air, plant your feet on the ground, and feel the sun shining down on you and quieting the noise in your head. Whenever you draw refreshed energy into your spirit body, the toxicity of the energy residue in your body diminishes as some of it naturally is released into your environment and back to the grid for recycling.

Whenever you acquire new residual energy from life experiences, or negative energy residue from your environment at a lower rate than you are expelling energy residue from your spirit body, your energy resonance improves. The more renewed energy that enters your spirit body, the lower the concentration of residual energy within you. However, if you have a lot of energy residue deposited within your spirit body, although energetically you appear "clean," your resonance still aligns with the energy residue stuck within you. Residual energy dust built up within your spirit body affects your ability to breathe energy effectively through your spirit body, thus negatively affecting your human trinity.

As your spirit body draws in energy and releases energy and energy residue, it too is "breathing." Instead of oxygen, it is energy from the universal energy grid or from the environment. As our spirit body "exhales," it releases energy residue out to the cosmos to be recycled into new energy. Most of us take our spirit body's ability to breathe energy for granted or just never think of the importance of it. However, if you consider what happens to the physical body if it cannot breathe oxygen, you know it can lead to significant brain damage and even death of our physical being. If our spirit body stops breathing energy, you will not die right away, but it has a dramatic effect on its ability to heal itself and replenish energy within you. Over time, you find that you drop lower and lower in deep sadness or apathy and reach a point where you are just going through the motions of living without gaining any joy from your life. This is a tragic place to be.

If you are interested in hearing your spirit breathe as it moves energy, try to pick a time when you do not feel heavy, tired, or sluggish. Most times when you are physically feeling worn down, tired, or emotionally exhausted, your spirit body is feeling the same way. In fact, it may be the source telling your physical body that your human trinity needs rest and a chance to replenish energy. At these times, your energy movement is going to be very slow and sluggish, which makes it difficult for you to hear or sense your energy movement. This can be frustrating if that is the time when you are trying to sense your energy movement. Instead, try to pick a time when your physical body feels rested, stirred up, or even angry. When you are angry or your energy is spinning, it is the easiest to sense or feel your spirit body energy within you. However, eventually, you will want to know how your spirit body feels as it breathes when you are rested and content. This is when you can experience how your energy moves in your normal "breathing" pattern. Although it is quieter than when you are angry or stirred up, it is what your energy feels like when you are in a steady state of energy movement and your spirit body is at peace. It is always a good thing to be aware of how your energy moves in its steady state.

To hear my energy move, I usually start with a meditation or yoga to calm the noise from my physical body and focus on my breathing. Once you are able to focus on your breath and are able to ignore the sound, then you can draw your energy inward. In this state, it is easier to attune yourself to hear your energy move within your spirit body. Just as our physical body moves oxygen into our body and expels carbon dioxide to breathe, which sustains life, our spirit body requires energy to sustain life. All spirit bodies have the ability to expel energy through any of their chakras, on their physical body's breath, or through their taproot. However, depending on the person, one might not be actually able to hear one's energy move. If you cannot hear your energy, try to focus on sensing its movement.

There are some similarities within the spirit body types in the general sound they make as they "breathe." There is a sound and sensation associated with moving energy in and out of our spirit bodies. Just as each of us has a unique breathing pattern, our spirit bodies also have variations in the sounds or sensations they make as they breathe energy. Even though you share the same spirit body type with another, the speed you move energy, the resonance of your spirit body, and your magnetism all enact subtle changes on the resulting 'sound' or 'feeling' when you are moving energy. For those of you who can sense or hear energy movement in others, you probably can also determine whether there is a blockage in another's spirit body energy. Some of you are able to figure out what caused the blockage based on the resonance of the energy residue clogging up a chakra or blocking the energy from moving. At times, it is far easier to sense shifts in another's spirit body energy than to sense shifts within yourself.

Regardless of whether you can hear it move or sense it, it does not matter. What is important is that you are actively "listening" to your spirit body move energy. This step is critical to helping you identify when there are blockages in energy movement. Blockages are similar to having a cold, bronchitis, pneumonia, or sinus infection. If you have an infection in your physical body's airways, it is more difficult to draw in the oxygen your body needs. Although you are still drawing oxygen into your physical body, it is more labored compared to when you do not have any type of infection. Your spirit body is very similar. Blockages in energy pathways do not stop you from "breathing energy." However, it can make the process more labored and challenging, especially if you are trying to navigate through a difficult life moment.

Depending on your spirit body type, how you move energy within it differs. Typically, the energy movement mimics the movement of the elemental energy we see in nature. We can see in our world that earth, fire, water, and air can and do behave differently, depending on the situation and circumstances. At any time in the world, these energy types can be calm or almost passive, to the other end of the spectrum, being wild, fierce, loud, and very strong to the point of being destructive. In considering how energy moves within your spirit body, keep in mind that your polarity and the shape of your sona affect the energy movement within your spirit body. Those of you with a loop pattern of energy movement through your spirit body tend to move energy in one predominant direction. If you have an infinity loop pattern, energy tends to move simultaneously in and out of your spirit body through at least one chakra and your taproot, generating a natural whirling of energy through you. It is almost like having a mini-cyclone of energy constantly pulsating through your spirit body.

When your spirit body draws in energy from the universal grid or the environment, it sounds or has a sensation similar to a heartbeat. As you know, when your heart beats, sounds are produced by the left and right ventricles, giving it the bum-bump sound. So too does the sound of energy moving through your spirit body. The strongest sensation is the new, refreshed energy drawn into your spirit body. The quieter sound or sensation is your spirit body "coughing" out some of the residual energy that has built up within it. Regardless of the spirit body type you have, all spirit bodies will organically draw in energy from the universal energy grid to replenish lost energy. However, if there are many blockages, the effectiveness of your spirit body in this process becomes challenging. As a result, the sound or sensation associated with the breathing pattern of your spirit body might be as soft as a baby's breathing as it sleeps to the loudest, most rumbling, gasping sound of a person who chronically snores, who could wake the dead if it were possible.

Those of your with an infinity loop sona tend to draw energy in from at least two sources at a time; the resulting sound or sensation of energy movement reminds me of the sound of a fetus's heartbeat inside of its mother. The loudest sound is from the energy moving in one direction. However, as the energy loops back through the infinity loop, there is an additional burst of energy as the spirit body draws in more energy through a secondary source. For some of you, it feels like an "echo" of energy movement as it travels through the opposite end of the infinity loop. This distorts the sound and sensation of energy movement within your spirit body and adds to the uniqueness of how your spirit body sounds when it breathes. If you draw in energy from your taproot as well as the throat chakra, it speeds up your energy movement regardless of your spirit body type. To simplify how energy moves within the spirit body, it is best to focus on how energy moves for those with a standard loop sona orientation. Just remember, if you have an infinity loop sona, there will be an echo of movement and sensation, making it a little more challenging for you to distinguish between the primary energy movement above or below where the sona twists.

EARTH ENERGY MOVEMENT

Of all the spirit body types, those with the earth spirit body tend to move their energy the slowest—almost methodically. Although they have the ability to move their energy quickly, it tends to have a much slower pace compared to other spirit body types when they are feeling calm. Their energy has a humming quality to it, and it resonates in the area of their base chakra. Some with earth energy can hear the hum or feel it when they focus on their energy movement. The energy movement can sound like a low growl as it moves or a keening sound when the earth energy is becoming angry or upset. When they are very angry, it feels like an earth tremor is ripping through their spirit body. This is the precursor of their releasing an energetic earthquake or volcanic eruption. When this occurs, the energy movement within their spirit body goes in a linear line straight up the chakras from the bottom to where it is released, which is usually the throat chakra.

Earth energy tends to move up from the taproot in waves of energy. If you can see energy move, it resembles how a wave moves across the surface of the ocean. Overall, the movement is slow from the root chakra to the top of the spirit body in waves of energy. Typically, their energy movement is faster at the base of their spirit body, and it is slower the higher you go. When earth energy people draw in universal energy or environmental energy on their breath, it pushes energy downward in waves towards their taproot. This type of energy movement promotes the growth of their taproot.

Earth energy people tend to move their energy in a linear fashion ... like a lava flow moving down a mountain. The energy feels thick and can feel heavy. The pace of movement is very steady and can feel slow. As it moves, the sensations within you are harder to perceive, since it tends to have a very gentle movement in the steady state. To trace the path of movement, it is easier to infuse a color with a specific energetic resonance that is easy for you to distinguish from your steady state into the energy you are drawing into your spirit body. As this energy moves, focus on the path it takes and the pace of the movement. While it is moving, try to sense the gentle suction this energy flow places on your spirit body, drawing in the residual energy and starting to carry it out on the energy stream.

FIRE ENERGY MOVEMENT

Those with a fire spirit body tend to move energy very quickly through their spirit bodies. Their energy roars though their spirit body as though it is in a rush to accomplish something ... anything. As fire energy rushes up from the taproot or in on your breath, it creates a lightning burst of movement. When it is moving in this way, it might be breathy or whooshing as it moves. The energy of a fire spirit body is like liquid fire that is speeding toward the other end of their spirit body. For those of you who can energetically see spirit bodies, their spirit body resembles a ball of fire in a quasi-human shape. Of all spirit body types, they can move energy the strongest the fastest. When those with a fire spirit body are calm, their energy pattern it is similar to a house on fire. As the energy moves, it licks up through their spirit body and there is a sensation of a low rumble of energy movement. It is similar to the sound of a fire happily burning through wood, devouring everything in its path. For some, the sound or feel of their energy as it moves has a snapping quality to it.

When these people are angry, their energy has a low, growling resonance or crackling noise and it feels like it is churning in their tummy. This is usually present when there is a danger of the fire spirit releasing fireballs of anger. At other times, their energy movement resembles a mushroom cloud blowing upward with a strong force; it collects at the top of the head region of their spirit body before mushrooming out and rolling back under the top of the mushroom. It reminds me of the mushroom cloud you see after an atomic bomb has exploded. If you can sense this in someone with a fire spirit body, most likely the person has just lost his or her temper.

Energy enters their spirit body from their taproot and forms a column of energy that moves upward through their chakras into their meridians in a quasi-linear path until it reaches the head region of the spirit body. At the same time, it sends some energy curling back down toward their base chakra, where it draws in more fuel to keep the fire going. This energy moves in a linear direction from the central energy column and shoots energy outward toward the edges of the spirit body. At times, their energy sparks off into the cosmos from their spirit body. It looks like a lit sparkler as it shoots off sparks in all directions. If this is happening, they are not grounding their energy well. When the energy is close to the heart chakra, the energy swirls inward. If the energy is moving slowly, people are stifled and feel restless; this state pushes them to seek out something in their environment to provide them with a burst of energy. People with fire energy can move their energy the fastest of all spirit body types, and they can almost spontaneously fill their spirit body with a huge burning ball of energy.

AIR ENERGY MOVEMENT

When people with air spirit bodies move their energy, it can be like a gentle breeze, fierce as a tornado, or something in between these two extremes of energy movement. Depending on the intensity of the movement, it can be very difficult for those with an air spirit body to sense their energy movement unless they are in a deep meditative state, or the energy is moving so fast it feels piercing and they do not even need to meditate to feel it. In their calm state, their energy movement is subtle and reminds me of someone breathing. It can be soft and gentle, or labored and gasping at the opposite end of the spectrum. When it is very light or wispy, it is very hard to sense. Although those with air spirit bodies can draw up energy through their taproot, their preferred source of energy is from their environment through their throat chakra. This is because it is faster for them to pull in energy on a breath than to meditate and focus on drawing air up through their taproot. This is the case unless, of course, they have been working on this process and use meditation or yoga to practice drawing in energy through their roots and are proficient enough to draw it in through either source quickly.

When air energy people draws in energy through their throat chakra, the energy splits, with some moving toward the head of the spirit body and the rest moving toward the base. This is a very efficient way to get energy to the top and bottom of their spirit bodies quickly. However, if they send too much energy toward their head and very little toward their root chakra, they might suffer from stress-induced migraines or headaches. If too much goes to their taproot and not enough through their brow or crown chakra, it translates into feeling stuck in life.

If you have an air spirit body, something to consider is that air energy tends to swirl and change directions very quickly. Therefore, it is more difficult to sense which way your energy is moving unless you use a color to tint it, making it easier to sense. Regardless of the strength of movement, air energy follows a pattern similar to blowing smoke. As it moves up, it curls around back on itself before joining another stream of energy while making its way through the spirit body. Usually, this energy moves in several directions simultaneously, with an overall movement from the throat to the crown chakra and a corresponding stream of energy from the throat to the root chakra.

The energy tends to stay in perpetual motion until it saturates all parts of their spirit body. Visually, it resembles a smoke-filled room with energy ebbing and flowing and in constant motion. As someone moves in the space, it stirs up the energy and the direction of the smoke changes briefly until it returns to its homeostatic pattern of movement. In your spirit body, as it moves through the spirit body, it stirs up energy residue caught in it. As the residual energy sweeps up into the energy movement, it briefly changes the direction or strength of the energy. Then the spirit body expels the energy residue on the "breath" or out of the taproot to return to the cosmos.

WATER ENERGY MOVEMENT

Those with a water spirit body tend to move their energy in a manner similar to the way water moves in nature. It can be as subtle as a trickling stream to the other end of the spectrum as a raging typhoon or hurricane of swirling energy. At times, the energy is laser-like in intensity, while at other times it curls and swirls as it moves. Regardless of the strength of the movement, it follows a distinct pattern. As it moves, you will sense energy spraying within you as well as ebbs and flows of rolling energy. Think of what the tide looks like on an ocean as it rolls onto shore. As it hits against the sand, small sprays of water burst up before quickly returning to the rolling water as it retracts back into the ocean. Within your spirit body, the energy does the same thing. When it moves, it causes all energy in the body to move forward, depending on the force of energy within your spirit body; it has small retractions of energy and rolls back toward the source of the energy, only to be pushed forward again as more energy is drawn into the spirit body. It is essentially taking two steps forward in pushing energy into the spirit body, followed by one step back, and the pattern continually repeats. When your spirit body is content, the energy movement tends to have a slow to moderate speed as it moves through the spirit body.

When water energy moves, it swirls, ebbs, and flows like waves breaking against the stones, rocks, or sand on a beach. As it moves, it stirs up energy residue within the body. In directing the energy to an outlet, the energy swell carries this energy on the tide. Going back to the analogy of an ocean, when the tide comes in, it creates waves of water that people can ride using surfboards. As energy residue is stirred up within your spirit body, the wave of energy picks it up and carries it to an outlet where it sprays out into the universal energy grid. This outlet might be your taproot, your breath, or the edge of your spirit body, where it is expelled into the cosmos.

An interesting phenomenon in large bodies of water is undertow. If you have a water spirit body, you too can suffer from undertow energy, which can pull you down energetically. This undertow can happen if you are going through a very difficult life phase and you have energy blockages limiting your ability to draw energy up into your chakras. When this is occurring, small tugs or blockages prevent the energy from easily moving up through your spirit body; this state causes a general sense of feeling down or energetically held back. Essentially, when your spirit body energy is being held back from nourishing itself with refreshed energy, this manifests in feelings in your physical body or emotions. It can also make it more difficult for you to release residual energy as the undertow keeps pulling it back into your spirit body.

CHAMELEON ENERGY MOVEMENT

Chameleons can move energy in a variety of different ways. The typical energy movement starts at the taproot, moving quickly up into their base chakra, and slowing down as it enters the middle layer of their spirit body. As the energy continues through their spirit body, it speeds up a little after passing through the core, back into the middle layer of energy. Then, once it reaches the top of the spirit body's upper layer, it speeds up again.

Depending on which layer of their spirit body is predominant at any given time, and whether chameleons are content, worried, or angry, the sound movement of their energy differs. If chameleons are calm, they can process incoming energy through any of the three layers within them. Through their innermost layer, their energy hums; if it is through their middle layer, it has a whooshing sound like the tide going in and out; and when it is through their outermost layer, it is more like a soft breathing. At first, you might hear a mixture of these sounds or sensations. Eventually, with practice, you should be able hear the sound from the layer that is predominant. Remember, if chameleons are sending energy through all layers, it is a symphony of energy that is like a melody playing within them when the three energy layers are contributing "noise" to the energy movement.

It is easier for chameleons to hear or sense their energy when they are upset, stressed, or angry. However, in these situations, their energy layers have begun to mix. When chameleons are angry and process the energy through their outer layer, it feels like steam rushing out of the spout of a kettle. If they process the anger through their inner layer, their energy sounds rumbling as though an earthquake is going to occur. If they release energy through their middle layer, chameleons can feel the energy as gurgling, red-hot energy rising up within their spirit body.

When they are upset, their energy swirls within the core of their spirit body, around the area of their navel before rising up in their spirit body. If they blow, the energy sounds like rushing energy and feels like a stream of burning energy blowing through the spirit body in a column straight up to the throat chakra. As the anger is dying down, it has a gurgling sound with an occasional snap as the energy continues to flow out but the ferocity of the energy movement has passed. Regardless of whether the energy is steam or fiery volcanic energy, chameleons can release this energy from the throat, brow, or crown chakra. Rarely do they release energy in anger from their heart chakra. Whenever chameleons release their angry energy as steam or a volcanic eruption, they also release tremendous amount of residual energy into the cosmos from their spirit body. However, the target of their anger can feel devastated by the force of the energetic release.

Depending on the life challenges the chameleon is experiencing, as the energy moves through the central core of the spirit body, the energy can feel stuck at times. If this is occurring, you might be able to sense the blockage or a slight bubbling sound as energy percolates through the spirit body. Some feel it as though they have a lump blocking the movement similar to the sensation of having something stuck in your throat. Moving their stuck energy from the core of their spirit body can be very difficult. There are times that a chameleon will bypass their core in order to avoid a blockage in a chakra. However, this is not in their spirit body's best interest. By doing so, they are starving the chakras located in the inner core of their spirit body of the energy it needs. To restore movement, the chameleon needs to draw in massive levels of energy to dilute their core of energy, making it less viscous, to allow the residual energy that is blocking movement to pass through it more easily.

SPIRIT BODY ENERGY MOVEMENT MEDITATION

Regardless of your spirit body type, your polarity, or the type of sona you have, when you are able to sense your energy movement, it allows you a greater sense of power and control over your spirit body and energy. It gives you a baseline to compare your energy to when life experiences are upsetting you. When you know what your steady state of energy movement feels like, it is far easier to determine whether or not you have work to do to restore energy movement that is being impacted by residual energy before it becomes a bigger problem for you.

In this meditation, we are going to focus on how the energy feels or sounds as it moves through your spirit body. To begin, find a quiet place to sit that is away from distractions, where you are comfortable and safe. You can sit on a chair or on the floor, with your legs crossed or in a lotus formation. If you prefer to lie down on a bed, a couch, or the floor, that is fine too. The most important thing is for your physical body to feel comfortable and relaxed. Now work your way through the following steps:

1. Start by visualizing your spirit body. If you can already see it, that's great! If you can't, visualize what you think yours would look like.

2. If you know how to do yoga breathing, do that. Otherwise, start focusing on your breath by inhaling through your nose. As you breathe in, mentally count to three and then breathe out through your mouth, counting to three or another number that feels comfortable and natural to you. When you inhale, feel your lungs slowly filling up to where they still feel comfortable, and then breathe out, releasing stress. Remember to listen to your body. At all times as you do this exercise, as you breathe, make sure your body feels comfortable and relaxed. The most important step is to shut down the internal noise in your head and to become more aware of your breath. If you feel uncomfortable in any way, you probably should not do this technique or wait until a later time when you do feel comfortable doing it.

3. Once you feel relaxed, visualize a white energy field that matches the shape of your body. If you do not happen to like the shape of your body, imagine a spirit body in any shape you want. You can even visualize your energy field in any color you want. If you are able to see your own aura, focus on your aura and the outer edge of the last color presented. Now you are ready to pull energy into your spirit body.

4. On an inward breath, pull in energy through the soles of your feet or through your base chakra, whichever is easiest for you. To decide, consider your physical placement. For example, if your feet are on the floor, then pull the energy up from the grid through your feet. If you are sitting on the floor or a pillow, then try pulling the energy in through your base chakra.

5. As you breathe, try to follow the energy as it moves through you. When you breathe out, send the used-up or old energy out through your mouth.

6. If you can see energy movement when you pull in energy through your spirit body, infuse it with a color to make it easier to follow.

7. On every breath, try to focus on your energy movement. If you sense energy flowing out from the chakras, this is your chakra energy. This means you are close to figuring it out.

8. Continue pulling in and sending out energy. Try sensing which way your chakras are spinning. If they send energy through your spirit body and into your third eye predominantly from the left, then you are spinning in a clockwise fashion. If the energy enters the third eye predominately from the right, then you are in a counterclockwise energy loop. If the chakra's energy directions are different in three or more energy centers, then you are out of alignment! If there is only one change of direction of chakra energy and it is around your solar plexus chakra, then you probably have an infinity sona.

9. Now pull in energy, push it through your spirit body, and follow it as it moves around, leaving on your exhaled breath.

10. As your energy moves, focus on how it feels or sounds as it is moving. Can you hear an echo when your spirit body breathes? Does it feel "hot"?

11. When you have finished this visualization, thank the angels and your guide for their help.

Chapter 10

ENERGY AND AURAS

One of the most important skills to learn is how to move energy through shared umbilical cords. Although we are quite good at passively moving energy from ourselves to those we love, we have the ability to send messages through the cords to specific people to whom we connect. In my book *Taking Back Your Joy of Living*, I explained how we form connections to those we love through energetic umbilical cords. These are similar to the physical umbilical-cord connection that a baby uses while in utero to obtain the necessary nutrients and release waste products during gestation. From the perspective of our spirit body, these connections link our spirit body to the spirit bodies of those to whom we connect.

The placenta filters and separates the baby's blood from that of the mother. In our physical state, our blood is our life source. Our spirit body's life source is energy that we can pull from the universal energy grid or from our environment. In respect to our energetic umbilical cords, we need to install filters to block the unwanted energy from others from entering our spirit body. As young children, we have some protection from our guides, who, with the help of the universe, install temporary filters in all cord connections to limit the energy entering our spirit body. It is our responsibility to decide to whom we want to connect rather than just connecting to everyone.

Before allowing a connection, we can use an energy litmus test to determine whether others resonate the same way we do. To test the resonance of another's spirit body, send a small burst of your energy from your spirit body at the spirit body of the other person. I typically send the energy out from my crown chakra. However, you can also send this energy burst from your throat chakra. If you already have an umbilical-cord connection with that individual, send the energy pulse through the cord, as long as the cord connects two like chakras. Consider using a colored energetic vibration before attempting this technique. If your energy is very similar to the other person's, it will be harder for you to determine which energy is your own unless you have a way of identifying it.

Where the energies mix, try to sense how the vibration or resonance of the other person's energy compares to yours. If you cannot tell the difference between your energies, then you are with a "like" person who is similar to you in many ways. When you sense a difference in vibration or resonance, try to determine the way the energy differs. Assess how the energy difference makes you feel. Consider whether the difference feels uncomfortable in any way, and reconsider whether you want to connect with the other. If you decide to connect, be certain to filter the cord connection to block any energy that does not resonate well with your spirit body.

AURAS

Your spirit body has a magnetism and resonance that some people see or sense. These resonances display in the form of energetic fog called an aura. Specifically, it is your spirit body's resonance manifested in subtle colors projecting beyond the confines of your physical body. In our human trinity state, we tend to translate energy resonance into a color, which is easier for our brains to understand and be able to describe. Each color has a different resonance. For many of you, if you see or wear a different color, it affects how you feel. This phenomenon also applies to auras, but in reverse. Our brains sense the resonance and then translate it into a color. This allows our brains to make sense of the energy resonance as something that is more tangible and concrete. The colors you perceive change depending on how much energy is moving through the chakras and how people feel, as well as whether or not they ground their energy. Depending on how well the energy is moving, the energetic resonance contributes to the colors displayed in your aura. Since every chakra in your spirit body emanates a color, if one chakra is emanating more energy into your spirit body than another, it affects the predominance of color seen in your aura.

At times, a chakra is stuck or not moving energy; then the corresponding energy resonance is nonexistent, and this chakra is not contributing any energy or resonance to the person's aura. How much the energy churns within a person, and the level of energy residue stuck within their spirit body, dictate whether the color in in their aura is translucent, wispy, murky, or opaque. Keep in mind, not everyone can see auras as colors. Instead, some of you might sense this energetic resonance or magnetism as a "feeling." Regardless of how you sense the resonance of another, being able to do so is a gift of your spirit body.

Whenever I have consciously looked at another's aura, the energy is in perpetual motion. Although the colors are distinguishable, the delineation of lines or layers of colors are not. Instead, the energy in the layers swirls into other layers, creating a beautiful free-flowing image. It reminds me of different colors of smoke moving around in a space. Sometimes, the colors intermingle, creating a new color, while at other times they are distinct. This collection of colors flows through the spirit body and radiates outside of the physical form, creating a bubble of energy around the person. Individuals who are in tune with their spirit body often resonate with purple-colored energy around the top of their head.

I have found that the farther you go from the center of the spirit body, the density and resonance of the spirit body often differs. I also find that the farther the energy is from the center of the spirit body, the more diffuse the aura color resonance becomes. Your aura is your energy signature that draws in similar energy from the universe. How your different energy centers resonate depends on the energy residue and energy held within your spirit body. If you hold in hurt and pain, they resonate through your entire human trinity and draw more of this negative energy into your life.

I have noticed that people who do not move energy through their chakras well tend to have a swirling energy on their uppermost energetic layer that has a "murky" feeling. If they are going through a tough time emotionally, their aura often resembles a continually churning storm cloud that is dark, menacing, and composed of varying shades of gray. If they are not grounding their energy, I see little flashes of energy that remind me of a thunderstorm, with dark menacing clouds that are throwing out flashes of lightning in every direction.

Another interesting thing I have noticed about auras is that when two people are engaged in a conversation, you can sometimes see their auras overlap. Depending on what they are talking about, the overlapping colors of the energy they are releasing can be any color combination. For example, if their resulting energy is dark and has a brooding or angry resonance, they are usually having some type of disagreement and they are both sending negative energy at each other or at a problem. Other times, it is a beautiful kaleidoscope of free-flowing energy. This happens when they are in agreement or are collaborating to try to solve a problem in a way that is in both of their best interests. When the auras are overlapping, they can almost read each other's mind, they are so in tune with each other. However, it is important to be cautious whenever you are overlapping auras with others, since energy transfer can occur during these periods. This is why it is so important to shield your spirit body, pull back your energy, and return the energy of others to them after the end of any type of interaction. This practice ensures that you have not picked up some of their energy residue over a situation that plagues your mind, causing you hurt, worry, or upset, even though it really is not your problem to solve.

When people are pulling in energy from the universe or are in tune with the ethereal world, the uppermost aura layer is a diffuse purple color with streams of silvery light. It is quite beautiful to see. Anyone can have this purple aura haze. However, it is more common to see this aura color surrounding psychics who access the Akashic records, clairvoyants, mediums, healers, yogis, or other spiritually attuned individuals as they are actively interfacing with energy.

Another interesting thing I have seen in auras is between people who love each other. This love does not even need to be the romantic kind. It is simply that someone loves another unconditionally and completely trusts the other, knowing that he or she is safe and cherished, and that the other will not betray him or her. When both people in the relationship are in this state, there are beautiful silvery threads of light that swirl up within their auras and wrap around the other. The ends of the silvery threads of light converge between the auras, creating a swirling silvery frame. In the center of this energetic frame is an orb of colored light that sometimes resembles a stone. The most common colors I have seen to date are pink, purple, a rainbow, or a white ball of moving energy. If it is pink and reminds you of rose quartz, it indicates that this relationship provides unconditional love, joy, and healing for the individuals at this time. It may be purple like amethyst, which indicates that this relationship provides comfort, peacefulness, and contentment.

When I see a rainbow in the center of the silvery threads, it reminds me of rainbow fluorite. From an energetic perspective, this energetic signature signifies that these individuals ground each other and boost each other's intuition and mental clarity as they go through their life experiences. When the silvery threads wrap around a white center, it makes me think of love that is unconditional and pure. This does not mean that the couple does not have disagreements. Rather, it indicates that the partners accept each other, faults and all. Regardless of the color of the center of the overlapping energy, whenever you see auras that wrap around another, it is a powerful indicator of love or attachment to the other. The color is only an indicator of the greatest gifts that the individuals gain from their connection. Even though the relationship appears to be a connection of opposites, whenever auras wrap around each other with silvery threads of energy, it means that they give each other what their souls need in their quest for growth, peace, and happiness in this lifetime.

TREE ENERGY AND THE SPIRIT BODY

The most important skill to learn is how to pull energy from the universal energy grid and into your spirit body. Depending on your spirit body type, the most effective method differs. However, we all share the ability to pull in energy when we are around large trees. If you are lucky enough to live near large trees, you might have found that somehow you feel more grounded when you are at home. A tree holds a perfect balance of energy. Within it, all of the four spirit energy types are present. The roots of the tree represent the earth spirit energies. The sap aligns with the fire spirit body. Next are the leaves in their ability to pull in carbon dioxide and release oxygen. Trees have the ability to transfer energy from the earth as well as from the sky.

Through its roots, a tree grounds itself, as well the roots being the primary connection to the Earth. The roots have a secondary purpose of drawing in nutrients, minerals, and water needed to sustain the tree's life. They are also instrumental in removing some of the waste products produced by the tree. The healthier the roots and the firmer the ground, the less likely it is that the tree will topple in a storm and have its roots violently pulled from the Earth. Earth energy spirits are similar to the roots of the tree and have a natural ability to ground their energy by spending time in nature or digging in the dirt.

The sap of a tree acts like liquid fire. Starting at the roots, it rushes through the tree, picks up essential nutrients, and carries them through the living tree to nourish it. Through the sap, waste products are captured and carried back down to the roots to be released into the Earth. The sap of the tree is much like the energy of a fire spirit. Their energy also moves very quickly, and those with a fire spirit body can send out energy in many different directions simultaneously. At times, it seems as though they are doing everything in a hurry, even though there is no reason for it. Spending time near large trees helps fire spirits ground their energy. Being near a tree can be a powerful way for fire spirits to de-stress if they consciously send their energy down and out their taproot as they relax or meditate.

The tree's leaves draw in carbon dioxide from the air, creating food for the tree, and as a result of photosynthesis, they release oxygen into the air. Through the leaves, the tree "breathes" … just like all human trinities breathe. Those with air spirit bodies, with practice, can effectively use air they breathe in, draw off the energy, and use it to expel the negative energy from their spirit body. Essentially, they can use the air to help ground their energy by ridding themselves of energy that is causing their spirit energy to spin. As the wind blows through the leaves of the tree, it reminds you to breathe more deeply. For air spirit bodies, breathing calmly and deeply helps the spirit body ground itself.

The final element is the water in the Earth and falling from the sky that nourishes the tree and is picked up by the roots and carried through the tree. All human trinities need water to survive. However, using water in a variety of forms helps those with water spirit bodies to ground their energy. Being around trees that are continually moving water energy acts as a gentle energy force within the water spirit body, encouraging the human trinity to release the negative energy.

CONNECTING TO THE DIVINE

Our spirit body also has the ability to connect to the ethereal world through our crown chakras. However, the physical noise within us and around us can make it difficult for us to connect and hear what the divine or those who have passed wish to share. Accomplished psychics, clairvoyants, and mediums tend to be more proficient in shutting out this noise to see past the veil with minimal difficulty. Essentially, they are able to calm their energy and activate their alpha waves while still being present in the moment. However, if you do not have these abilities, it can be more challenging to achieve these connections with the ethereal world while you are actively interacting with others in the physical world.

If you are not particularly psychic, you can still learn how to connect with the divine and activate your spirit body's ability to communicate with the ethereal world. The most important first step is to find a way to calm the noise around us, and within us. One way to achieve this is through meditation. When we meditate and quiet the physical distractions, we allow the alpha waves to take over. Depending on the channel you access during the period when alpha waves are prevalent, you will find yourself in a lovely daydream, talking with your guides, or connecting to the ethereal world. The most important thing is to clear your mind of all conscious thought and accept the incoming information without trying to change it or interpret it. Then at the end of the meditation, write everything down. That way, if you want to analyze the information, you do not need to worry about forgetting something.

When the alpha waves take over, some people will immediately start daydreaming of what they wish would happen or how a situation will turn out. Sometimes the act of visualizing a positive outcome helps you step outside of a stressful situation to provide you with a calm respite from stress, allowing you to regain focus and strength to continue. If you are in this situation, remember that it is not in your best interest to spend all of your time in a daydream to avoid the stresses in your life. Your soul is on a mission. Spending too much time dreaming of what can be without doing something to make positive changes in your life will not help your soul in its quest.

Others will find that they can connect with their guides when their alpha waves are active. During this time, their guides answer the questions that have been plaguing their mind when they were seeking direction or guidance. It can be deeply moving for some people when their guides confirm that they need to take steps that are going to be difficult for them to do. When your guides are sharing tough messages that something will not turn out just as you want it to, it can be very upsetting, especially if you were hoping for a happy conclusion for everyone. If their message helps you release some emotional pain that you have bottled up inside, you may find that at the end of this state you burst into tears and sob as though your heart is breaking. This can be cathartic for your spirit body as it rids itself of the negative energy that was stuck within it. Remember, guides give you advice on how to manage yourself through a difficult situation. They do not tell you what to do. If a spirit is telling you what to do, there is a very good chance that it is the spirit of someone who has died that is posing as your spirit guide. Always consider the potential impacts on following through on their advice to avoid causing harm to others or yourself.

Another energetic wavelength your spirit body can tune in to is the ethereal plane. While the alpha waves are prevalent, with practice, you can communicate with the ethereal plane to gain help, guidance, information, or reassurance that you are on the right path. This is when you can connect to the divine to find answers to the bigger questions. However, you will receive guidance, but rarely will they tell you that you must do anything unless your human trinity is in dire jeopardy if you do not act immediately to resolve something. At all times, the universe honors the gift it gave you of free will to choose your actions. Once we end the connection, our spirit body automatically shares much of what we have learned with our physical body. The knowledge, insight, and wisdom our spirit body acquires in this state is accessible to our mind, allowing us to choose whether we want to act on it.

When connecting to the ethereal world, your spirit body can tune in to the frequency of the Akashic records to learn more about your past lives. Here you can seek the answers to questions on why you do certain things even though they do not make any sense in your current lifetime. For example, you might suffer from claustrophobia but you don't know what triggered this fear. By accessing the Akashic records, you will learn what happened in a past lifetime that is affecting you today. In this case, it might be that in a past lifetime, someone locked you up in a tiny space for a very long time and you struggled trying to escape. This past-life memory written in your soul might be the reason why you react to small spaces today.

We can also tune in to the ethereal world to talk with the angels. This is where I learn much of what I know today about who we are, why we matter, why we need each other, and how to protect our spirit body from harm, as well as a host of other information. When communicating with the angels, you need to be very careful on your resonance. If you resonate positively or with a pure heart, you can easily connect to the good angels such as Archangel Michael, Archangel Gabriel, and others like them. If you are resonating negatively or your heart is not pure in intent, there is a chance you will connect with spirits who possess negative intent that pose as angels.

Regardless, whenever you connect to entities claiming to be "good" angels, be very careful to assess the information before following their advice. What they tell you to do or the information they give you may not be in the best interest of your human trinity or of humanity. The most important thing to do is to run the information and the resonance of the entity you are communicating with against your spirit body energy to determine whether it resonates in the same way as you do. This should give you an indication of it came from a good or bad information source. Unfortunately, if you ask angels if they are angels, they will say yes. However, they usually do not volunteer whether they are good or not. Even the "bad" ones when asked will lie and indicate that they are "good" angels. Remember, they get to practice their own free will just as we do.

In this state, you might want to try communicating with people you loved who have passed. Remember, even though you are ready to communicate with them, they may be otherwise engaged and will not connect with you. My suggestion is that if you plan to connect to someone who has passed, put it out to the universe first that you plan on connecting. This can be as easy as saying, "On Friday I plan to try connecting to XXXX, who has passed." Doing this gives them advance warning you want to connect. Think of it as though you are making a coffee date. Would you expect friends to meet you at a coffeehouse in a different city on a specific day and time without telling them to meet you there? The chance of them being there is remote. However, if you let them know ahead of time you plan to connect, you will have a better chance of making your connection with them. The same applies to those who have passed. Whenever I want to meet up with the spirits of deceased loved ones, I send out a message through the residual cord connection, or say aloud when I plan on connecting. This gives them the chance to meet up with me. Otherwise, they might be busy visiting another relative when I was reaching out to chat with them.

There are times when you want to connect with people who recently died. If people you want to meet with are newly departed and passed more than fourteen days previously, and it is less than six months since they passed, you probably will not be able to connect with them unless they lived the life of a saint. During this time, they are experiencing their purification process, going through their life's debrief and watching how their actions affected the lives of others. When they are in this state, you will not be able to communicate with them. This period can last upwards of a year after they passed. If they committed suicide, this period is much longer. Unfortunately, people who commit suicide need to work through what they were supposed to do in this lifetime. Until that process finishes, they are unreachable. In addition, if souls are getting ready to start their next journey or they have embarked on it, you will not be able to communicate with them either. If you are lucky, they will communicate with you before they enter the body for their new life to let you know that they are moving on.

One of the gifts of your spirit body is its ability to "travel." Although your spirit body is tethered to your human trinity through the sona, it has the ability to reach up to the divine and to communicate with angels. Some of you have additional spirit body gifts that make travel to the divine easier to accomplish than it is for others. Regardless, everyone has the ability to communicate with the divine, and the more you practice, without trying to force it, the easier it becomes. As you meditate and quiet the mind, your spirit body reaches up to the heavens to seek out divine knowledge or understanding. In this state, we are in communication with the divine energy of all life. Some of you pray to reach this connection with universal energy. Regardless of how you achieve it, your spirit body is reaching up for knowledge, inspiration, guidance, assistance, or anything else that you wish to manifest in your physical state or in your life. In this state, your spirit is lifting within your human trinity. This can result in the base chakra of your spirit body resting at the eyebrow level of your physical body.

Not everyone needs to meditate or pray to achieve a state that enables his or her spirit body to travel. Some of you travel in your spirit body as you sleep. Although you are very much alive, your physical body is in a deep sleep state and your alpha waves are prevalent. While in this state, your spirit body can interact with the souls of loved ones who have passed. If you ever meet up with deceased loved ones in this state, try not to focus on the fact that they have died in the physical sense. Instead, take the opportunity to talk to them and ask them the questions that you really need them to answer. I once wasted an opportunity to talk to a loved one who visited as I slept because I was so focused on the fact he was no longer with me in the physical sense. Those who have passed know they are dead in the physical sense. I comfort myself with the knowledge that I had the opportunity to hug him and kiss him one last time. Although I can communicate with those who have passed, it is not every day that I have the opportunity to embrace the spirit of someone who passed in that way.

In this dream travel state, you can also meet up with the spirit bodies of loved ones, friends or even enemies as they too are traveling. Remember, if you engage in a fight in this state, you are still responsible for the energetic outcome of what you did. As your spirit body travels, you will receive divine inspiration on how to handle a situation, or esoteric knowledge or answers to questions you have asked the universe. Other times, you may meet with people you have not met in the physical state. Then, a short time later, you meet them. Whenever this happens, pay very close attention to what you learned in the traveling state. If they were friends in their spirit body form, they are friends in the physical as well. If not, watch your back. The angels may have set up the meeting in the traveling state to show you their true intention as a warning to give you a chance to protect yourself.

If you are in a dreamlike state when your spirit body travels, it isn't a good idea for another to try to wake you. The only time you may be in jeopardy of passing is if you have traveled too far and someone is trying to wake the physical body and your spirit body cannot completely reintegrate itself fast enough, causing it to disconnect from your sona. Once this happens, the sona tears open, releasing your soul, and your human trinity will disintegrate. Thankfully, this does not happen very often. Usually, if your spirit body is traveling and someone tries to wake your physical body, although your entire spirit body superimposes itself back on top of the physical body, the alignment can be off. For the remainder of the day, or until you meditate, you might feel off, out of your skin, or slightly disoriented in some way. Some may even feel like their head is "swimming" or suffer from light vertigo. For others, it is like putting on a dress shirt that is inside out and backward. It just does not feel as comfortable as it does when it is worn the right way. Your spirit body feels equally uncomfortable if it has not realigned itself correctly within your human trinity.

THE POWER OF LOVE ENERGY

Love energy is a powerful form of energy that infuses your spirit body with the energy of others. Since their energy is new and often has a difference resonance than your own, you might experience it as a powerful aphrodisiac. Love energy can feel as though it protects your spirit body from unintentional attacks from the loved one with whom you are sharing this energy. However, over time, as your spirit body acclimates to this energy, the ability of this energy to cushion your spirit body from little hurts diminishes. Initially, new love energy can numb your spirit body from the attacks and damage that others do to you. However, it does not protect you from attacks from others.

Energetically, it creates a temporary "love bubble" when you are distracted and are not as aware of the extent of the damage that is being done to your spirit body. Even though you are oblivious to your surroundings and you are viewing life through rose-colored glasses, it is not protecting you. Rather, it might leave you in a place where you do not shield yourself adequately, making you more vulnerable to energy attacks. The danger of new love is if you feel impervious to negative energy attacks, the effectiveness of new love energy is often very short-lived, and it cannot protect your spirit body. Although love energy is great, it is not enough to protect you or heal your spirit body from damage.

The more your energy differs in resonance or types of residual energy, the better the infusion of energy can feel because it is so different. This feeling can generate a false sense of strength and protection that is not there. For some, it creates a false sense that nothing can or will go wrong. Love can feel like it sustains you; or feeds you. However, this is an illusion. Although love energy feels powerful it does not protect you. At times, love from the wrong person can be so distracting that you miss the signs that your spirit body is in trouble and needs urgent help to protect itself from harm. Your ability to protect your spirit body comes from managing your energy and placing shields around it to deflect energetic attacks from others. Protection can also come from the universe, from your guides and sometimes from the angels.

As you acclimate to the love energy, the resonance might be so different from yours that it is toxic to your spirit body. When you resonate similarly, you can grow together. When you resonate differently, it can pull your spirit body in a direction that you did not intend to go. Once the love fog wears off, you may discover that you do not like the person you are beginning to be or that the person you are with aren't who you thought they were. While they are in the love fog, some find that they have been unconsciously tearing away cords from others whom they love in favor of the new love, which has taken all of their focus. This might mean that when you realize that you are in trouble, you have crippled your human relationship matrix to the point that you have only a couple of people you can pull on to give you strength to get through the difficult process of taking back your life.

When the love energy is good for you, it can be a catalyst pushing you toward your becoming the best version of who you are. Together, you help each other better yourselves, learn, and grow. Your human relationship matrixes grow as you include the loved ones connected to your partner within your own matrix. Remember, it is rare that a relationship that takes you away from your human relationship matrix is in your spirit body's best interest. However, sometimes your resonance improves because this new love helps rid your spirit body of energy residue. This might mean that you grow away from those in your human relationship matrix who have been holding you back from following your soul's energy work. This tends to more likely if you have been leaving behind destructive relationships that were causing you to do things that were mean or hurtful, or caused harm to others. Any relationship that causes you to become more negative or hurtful to others typically is not in your soul's best interest. In essence, that relationship is bringing out the worst version of you to act in the world around you, which may be contrary to your soul's mission to overcome this way of being in this lifetime.

Chapter 11

YOU AND YOUR ENERGY

Your energy is a wonderful gift from the universe, and you should always try to make the most of it in your life. Using it, you have the ability to manifest good things in your life. You can also use it to draw like-minded people to you while distancing yourself from those who are energetically draining you. Energy is a gift that is continuously flowing and replenishes within your spirit body—as long as you remember to pull in energy from the universal grid or allow yourself to enjoy time spent in an energetic zone that complements your spirit body. Through our spirit bodies we interact with our environment and those within it. Wherever we go, whatever we do, we leave an energetic trail or residual energy dust indicating that we were there—unless we pull back our energy. As I mentioned earlier in this book, this energy is on the DNA that your body has shed during the day. We also leave behind traces of energy that we have released from our spirit bodies as we engage with others in our lives.

ENERGY SIGNATURE/SPLATTER

Everywhere you go, you leave behind an energetic signature that resonates with your human trinity. Consider what happens when you walk through mud and then walk through your home. If you look back on where you walked, you will see traces of the wet mud left behind on the floor. Another example is when children have paint on their hands and touch walls and doors. Even though they are trying to be very careful, and the paint is partially dry, you will see small amounts of paint everywhere you look. It is the same with our energy. Every day, we leave behind traces of our DNA in the form of dead skin, hair, saliva, and even fingerprints. No matter how hard you try, unless you cover up your entire body, there is a chance you will leave genetic material pulsating with your energy wherever you go.

The same thing happens with energy from our spirit body. Everything we do, think, or say releases energy into our environment. Although we cannot see it with our naked eye, this energy is there and is pulsating with our energy signature. If we had the ability to see it under a fluorescent green light, you would see splatters of energy residue you left behind in the entire place. It would be the same as looking at an object through a microscope after a day of people touching it. Although with your naked eye you could not see the skin cells, bacteria or viruses on it from the people who touched the object, under the microscope it would be visible. Your energy is the same. Although you are not be able to see the traces of the energy you left behind, it is on almost everything you touched during the day. You will also see the energetic splatter from anyone else who was in the space who did not recall his or her energy either. No matter how much you physically clean a space, unless you clear the energy as well, the energy residue remains.

ENERGY IN YOUR HANDWRITTEN WORDS

Whenever you write anything on paper or on any other surface, you are leaving your intent and energetic resonance behind. This can be a powerful sample of your energy. The power of this energy comes from several sources. As you write, your brain processes what you are going to write; it transfers energy to the hands to move the nerves and muscles to write. Any emotion you have has an energy resonance aligning with your energetic state the moment you wrote on the paper. This essence transfers into the written word on the paper. Additionally, as you write, your brain communicates with your spirit body, and it releases energy associated with your intent. Therefore, anytime that your sign your name or write someone else down, you are infusing it with the energetic essence from both your physical and spirit bodies. Anyone who knows how to harness this energy can do something as innocuous as directly connecting to you. However, some try to use this trace of your energy if they want to cast curses, hexes, or other negative wishes against you.

Therefore, it is critical that you remove your energy from anything that you have written, regardless of the medium upon which you wrote. This also includes painting or anything that you create using your hands. Additionally, if you made anything that drew blood at the time you made it, even though you wiped away the blood, the energetic resonance is magnified. If you handle paper, you know how quickly you can get a paper cut. My recommendation is that if you cut yourself on a piece of paper, destroy it rather than giving it to anyone else. By giving it to someone, you are giving your tacit approval for him or her to use the energy on it, which might not be what you intended to do. For more about your DNA, refer to the chapter on DNA in this book.

PULLING BACK YOUR ENERGY

One of the most important skills to learn is how to pull back your energy from a space, person, or even something you wrote on but forgot to remove your energy from at the time. Whenever you leave energy behind, it is a direct link back to your spirit body. If you are proficient in moving your energy, simply call it back. Once you do, it will repatriate. It is always a good idea to ask the universe to destroy any energy residue connected to energy you are pulling back before it enters your spirit body. Another option is to send it back to the universal energy grid to be recycled. I tend to do the latter if my energy was partially used up in some type of interaction or if I am not sure if someone has connected to my energy. To send energy back to the universe, simply tell your energy to leave the space and return to the universal energy grid. Regardless of whether you call your energy back or send it to the universal energy grid, you may find that you need to use an object or complete an action to help you focus your intent.

If you are physically removed from the location where your residual energy is, you can still pull back your energy. Before beginning, you need to sit or stand in a position in which you feel completely comfortable. Then ground your energy using any approach you prefer. Once you feel grounded, draw in energy from the grid. Consider the type of energy you left behind. What chakra aligns the closest with it? Once you can visualize the energy, you are ready to pull back your energy. While in a calm state, twirl a finger in the air three times in front of the chakra that aligns closest with the energy left behind. Then flick your finger toward yourself. As you do this say, "All of my energy that remained in XXXX returns to me, and any energy from anyone else that has connected to it returns to the universal energy grid for recycling." When you are doing this, you are sending out the request from the chakra that aligns with the energy, using its magnetism to make it easier to draw back the energy. If you are not sure which chakra aligns the closest with the energy left behind, twirl a finger in the air three times in front of your throat chakra.

If you are not sure if you pulled back all of your energy, you can send energy to shield the residual energy from detection. At times, you might have been spewing energy all over the place in a burst of anger. In this situation, it can be more difficult for you to pull back all of your energy. After pulling back as much as you can, you can destroy any of your energy left. To do this, ask the universe to engulf any residual energy that you left behind in an impenetrable bubble of energy and then this bubble immediately self-destructs, destroying the residual energy and return it to the energy grid. This process will make it more difficult to trace it back to you. However, it is always more effective to call your energy back or send it to the universal energy grid for recycling. If you are concerned that you left energy behind, ask the angels or the universe for help to remove it and turn it into dust before returning it to the universal energy grid for recycling.

SHAKING OFF NEGATIVE ENERGY

Sometimes the energy you want to remove is from someone else or from a group of people. If you have just left a physical location where a lot of negative energy was blasting around you, and it feels as though some is clinging to your spirit body, you might want to shake off this energy before leaving. There are a few ways to do this. The first is at the street or sidewalk in front of the property. Once you have exited the property, stamp a foot lightly three times. You do not want to stamp it so hard that you hurt yourself. It also does not matter which foot you use. As you do it, say, "All of the negative energy that is clinging to me remains in this place." This energetically causes the residual energy to drop off your spirit body as though it was just demagnetized. If you struggle to stamp your feet, you can also accomplish this by tapping a cane or crutch against the ground three times. If you are in a wheelchair, tap your hand on a wheel of your wheelchair. You could even tap your hands together three times if you choose. Regardless of whether you use your foot, cane, crutch, or hand, your intent will flow through the medium and it will demagnetize the energy, causing it to fall away.

You may want to consider shaking off residual energy when you are moving out of a space to a new home. As you prepare to move, a lot of disruptive energy is released. Residual energy is stirred up as you rediscover objects containing strong energy, regardless of whether it elicits a positive or negative emotion from you. As you are boxing up your former life to move your stuff, it can also elicit feelings of sadness, melancholy, or a host of other feelings. Every feeling releases energy into your environment.

One approach to shake off this energy before moving your belongings to a different home is to sage the space before you start packing, partway through the packing, and again after you finish packing. Using the sage will force the residual energy back to the universal energy grid. Another approach can be used as you are packing and before you seal up each box. With the box still open, wave your hand above it in a circle; then once you close the circle, draw you hand upward. As you do this you say, "Any residual energy from this home that is on these items, leave my belongings and return to the universal energy grid for recycling." Then immediately seal the box. A final step is to give the place a thorough cleaning to remove any residual energy from your time in this space. As you clean, place your intent on the cleaning solution or vacuum, that it removes the residual energy and sends it back to the grid for recycling. The benefit of doing this is that it makes it harder for the next resident to connect to you afterward.

SIPHONING ENERGY

There are times when you connect to people who are experiencing a tsunami of energy in their spirit body or are in the throes of a very painful emotional situation. At times, someone in your human relationship matrix is going through a stressful time and needs help to ground his or her energy because it is spinning out of control. This loss of control can be the result of their going through a painful breakup, stressful situations at work, or any other situation where they feel that their emotions are taking control over their body and they are left struggling to handle the resulting influx of energy. If you are able to see chakra energy, you will notice that one or more of their chakras are pulsing with energy or feel engorged with an excess influx of energy. It may even look like it is ready to shatter. You might be worried that they are struggling to cope, and you might be afraid for their safety; they may need to get home or to a safe place and siphon off some of this excess energy. The benefit for them is that by pulling off the excess energy, they have a better chance of thinking more clearly and will be better able to focus their minds.

Before attempting to pull off other people's energy when they are imploding, you should have their permission to do so. Getting this permission can be as simple as asking them if you can draw some of this chaotic energy from them. If they say no, then you must comply no matter how badly you want to help them. If you do not comply, then you are interfering with their free will to manage their own energy in the way in which they choose. However, there are times when they are not even in the right headspace to agree to someone helping them. Although you should not pull on others' energy without permission, the universe may expressly give it to you on their behalf. Remember, if the universe is giving you permission to do this, you do not need to ask for it. When I get this type of direction, there is literally a divine sign to do it. It can be a ray of sunshine shining down on them, casting others into a faint shadow as though the universe has just placed a spotlight on them. Whatever sign the universe uses, I tend to receive some type of physical sign above or around them that is pointing directly at them, singling them out from the crowd. I find that the universe is quite ingenious at pointing them out. When the universe is directing you to draw off this energy, you can do it for a short period without reprisal from karma or the universe. Once you have permission from the person to help him or her, you need to determine the strength of the energy that you are going to try pulling off and whether your spirit body can handle it. The nice thing when the universe or a good angel gives you permission is that you know you can handle the load of energy; the universe never would have asked you to do it if you did not have the ability to do so.

Consider the wiring of a house. If you have 200-amp service and the energy draw is 199 amps, then the wiring pulling in the energy can handle the energy. However, if you have 60-amp service and try to pull 199 amps of energy, the wiring cannot handle it and you can cause problems with the electrical system of the house. The same applies to your spirit body. If your spirit body wiring allows you to pull massive amounts of energy, you can easily siphon off excess energy from others without harmful effects. If their energetic wiring can handle more energy than your spirit body, and their energy is stronger or moves faster than you can easily handle, you can quickly end up pulling so much energy that your spirit body cannot handle it. The result of attempting to siphon off their energy is that you will short out your own energy, throwing your spirit body into a spin.

It might be tempting to think that if another can pull off massive amounts of energy from others, so can you. However, you need to be very honest with yourself about your energetic abilities to avoid hurting yourself before siphoning energy for another. If your spirit body is not equipped to move and hold the energetic load, you can cause issues with its ability to move energy through it. Regardless of how much you care for others and want to help them, if you short out your spirit body, it can manifest as electrical issues within your physical body when your spirit body shares information through the two-way communication system. Therefore, it is always best to limit how much energy you try moving to protect your human trinity. In reality, it is not conducive to your spirit body's health if you can help one person, destroy yourself, and limit your ability to help another in the future.

Interestingly, I have found that those with an earth or chameleon spirit body tend to be more adept at siphoning large amounts of energy from others, while those with an air or fire spirit body are more likely to harm themselves to some degree. My suspicion is that this issue relates to the way they try moving the energy. Simply put, those with a fire or air energy spirit body may accidentally move the energy through their own spirit body. Doing this will cause energy issues within their own spirit body. For those with a water spirit body, their effectiveness depends on the density of their spirit on the day when they want to siphon the energy and their approach. If you have a chameleon spirit body, you can pull the energy through a second cord connection you create that attaches to your uppermost layer and run it off the outside of your spirit body to return to the cosmos. This may mean that some of your energy layer will burn off in this area of your spirit body as you move the energy away from your loved one. If you choose to do this, expect to feel tired afterward and to need to draw in more energy to replenish the energy you burned up. My recommendation is to use your energy to draw the energy from another, but block their energy from entering your sprit body in any way. That way, you lessen the chance that the energetic load of spinning energy will negatively affect your spirit body. Regardless of your spirit body type, whenever you allow energy to pass through your spirit body, you increase the likelihood of causing damage to your spirit body.

Additionally, you need to know how much energy they usually have. When siphoning off energy, you want to pull off only the excess energy. You do not want to take so much energy that they do not have enough energy left to effectively manage their human trinity. If you have determined that you can safely siphon their excess energy and you have more than one shared umbilical cord, you need to decide on the cord to use to draw the excess energy. The best cord to use is one that you create specifically for this purpose. Typically, if I siphon energy, I create a new cord for the sole purpose of siphoning energy to protect the primary cord connections. If you are a chameleon, create a cord connection to the uppermost layer of your spirit body. When creating a new connection, try to align the connection that attaches to the same chakra in both of your spirit bodies. Remember, you had permission to establish the first one, so it is okay to make a second cord connection. When you make this connection, try to connect no higher than the throat chakra. When I use this technique, my preference is to start at the throat chakra, since it is closest to their third eye and crown chakra; spinning energy usually originates in these chakras before spreading to the lower chakras. Depending on how the strength of the energy whirling through them or if the individual is a worrywart, trying to siphon their energy may cause an energetic earthquake within their spirit body that can have significant negative effects on their energy and in their life.

Now you need to create an outlet to dispose of the energy without allowing it to enter your spirit body. In the secondary cord or newly formed cord, install an energetic hole just before it attaches to your chakra, and then create a funnel that attaches to the hole. The small end of the funnel connects to the cord and the largest end of the funnel is open to the cosmos. This configuration allows the energy to drop into the cosmos instead of it entering your spirit body. Then install a solid filter at your chakra where the cord connects to your spirit body with your intent that it blocks all of the energy you are going to siphon from entering your spirit body; diverting the energy to the funnel you installed to empty directly into the cosmos. Instill your intent that it allows for a one-way transmission of energy from them to you but the energy does not enter your spirit body. Within this cord, install the intent that you can pull only the negative, swirling energy from them. All positive and good energy they have in their spirit body stays with them and cannot pass through the cord. They are already in the throes of emotional and energetic pain. They need every little bit of good energy they have.

In the primary cord connections, ask the universe or your preferred angel who helps you to fill the cord with dense white light that blocks all energy movement. This step prevents you from receiving a backwash of negative residual energy into your spirit body as you are siphoning energy. Then turn your attention to the cords of the loved one from whom you want to siphon energy. Ask the universe to fill all cord connections to him or her with dense white light to stop all energy movement for the duration of the siphoning to prevent transference of energy accidentally to others. This step prevents you from accidentally pulling energy from someone your loved one also shares a cord with who does not directly connect to you. If you have the gift of amplification, turn your energetic megaphone to de-amplify energy. Once the energy enters the cord, send the de-amplification energy into this cord to shrink the siphoned energy to conserve your energy and make it easier to send their chaotic energy back to the universal grid.

After deciding which cord you will use to pull the energy, you are ready to begin. As with any energetic technique, start by placing your physical body in a comfortable position, whether it is sitting, standing, or lying down. Then close your eyes and focus on your breathing. Draw your focus inward, and feel the energy move through your spirit body. Since you will be using your taproot to expel the unwanted residual energy created within your spirit body from your used up energy as you do this, be sure to draw new energy in through your crown chakra or your throat chakra on each breath. Focus on drawing in this positive energy and pushing it through your spirit body and out of your taproot.

Using this energy, create an energy vacuum to siphon energy through the only active cord. This energy also provides the energetic pressure behind the negative energy you are siphoning that forces it back out of your spirit body and into the universal energy grid. Feel the strength of this energy as it moves through you and pushes residual energy in your spirit body to the grid. This is an important step to neutralize the magnetism of your energy body to prevent some of your loved one's negative residual energy from sticking to you as you move his or her energy. Once you feel that your energy is neutral, you are ready to move to the next step.

Gently pull on the person's energy and draw it into the new secondary cord connection. Using the energy from the grid, create a constant energetic pressure to draw out his or her excess energy from their spirit body. As you start pulling their energy, divert it to the location where you are going to expel the energy back to the universe for recycling. Consider infusing this energy with a color to ensure that your energy does not leave with the expelled energy.

As you are moving the person's energy, you may feel your spirit body protesting a little about the amount of energy you are using up during this technique. Be sure to continue pulling energy from the grid to create the vacuum that pulls in his or her energy while it also pushes out any energy that accidentally enters your spirit body and returns it to the universal grid. Continue this process until you feel that the influx of negative energy has diminished or you begin to feel energetically tired. Once you have decided to stop siphoning your loved one's energy, ask the angels to fill the cord with dense white light starting at both ends of the cord. As the white light moves closer to your spirit body, visualize that it is sending any remaining energy that is still in the cord out of the hole you installed earlier. Then ask the angels to neutralize any energy remaining in the cord and to stop all energy movement. Once all energy movement through the cord has ceased, continue to pull in positive energy from the grid through your crown or throat chakra. Push out any residual energy created during this procedure from your spirit body and return it to the grid.

You probably should consider installing a filter on it, close to your spirit body, that blocks all energy through it unless you need to use it again. Then ask the universe to remove the dense white light from all cords except for the one used for siphoning. Using your third eye, validate whether the dense white light has left all of the applicable cords and they are functioning as they did before. Be sure to add filters in the active cords to block any residual energy that was stirred up within them from entering your spirit body. After finishing, thank the universe and the angels for helping you help your loved one. I do this by saying "thank you" seven times in a row.

If any of the siphoned energy enters your spirit body, you need to send it straight out of your taproot back to the universal grid for recycling. Never keep this energy. It is full of negative residual energy as well as active chaotic energy. Additionally, if you keep it to use it in any way, you are in essence acting as an "energy vampire." The problem is that this energy is so chaotic it can cause serious disturbances in your spirit body. If it is full of energy residue from your friend, then you too will begin to experience the emotional turmoil that he or she is experiencing. If you begin to spin, it is going to make it much harder to help the person. From the perspective of loved ones, if they are sensitive to energy movement, they might feel that you are siphoning energy from them. As the energy moves, they should start feeling numb from an energetic perspective. As you siphon energy, depending on where you have connected, energy is pulled from the chakra to which you connect, then from the chakras immediately below or above it, and finally to all chakras within their spirit body. When the chaotic energy is leaving them, they often sense a feeling of calm or that they are in a dreamlike state. Some feel an overwhelming sense of calm.

Those who are very sensitive to their energy will notice that you have not taken any of their positive energy. Once the recipient of this technique reaches a neutral balance of energy in their spirit body, they should have already noticed that the volume of energy has diminished and the vacuum isn't pulling on their energy as strongly as before. This leaves recipients of this kind of energetic intervention feeling energetically or emotionally numb. Although they can think and process information, they are not "with it" and feel slightly distanced from their spirit body. This is an indication that the person who siphoned their energy in the energetic crisis did his or her job very well.

If someone has siphoned energy for you, remember, this is only a short-term fix. Once he or she has finished, be sure to ground yourself as soon as you can. Remember to install a shield if you need additional protection, infuse it with color to pull in specific intent or strength from the universe, and take back control of your energy. By siphoning off this energy, your loved one has given you an energetic gift to rebalance yourself at his or her energetic expense. In some situations, you may not even know who pulled off this chaotic energy. If a stranger did this for you, be sure to thank him or her. However, if you are able to determine who drew the energy from you, also be sure to thank the universe for stepping in to help you when you needed it most.

STOPPING SPINNING ENERGY

There are times when each one of us "spins" energetically. Sometimes this spinning energy comes through a primary cord connection. Whenever someone who connects to you through a primary cord connection begins to spin, there is a small tugging sensation on the energy within your spirit body. When you feel it, you can either filter the cord to stop all energy movement or try to stop the person's spinning energy. I must warn you, stopping the spinning energy of another is difficult and can result in a strong backlash of energy into your spirit body. This energy in turn can cause you to spin or to experience an energetic earthquake. Be sure to approach this technique with caution.

From an energetic perspective, what you are doing is the equivalent of sticking a rod into a moving bicycle wheel. This is a very dangerous thing to do for everyone involved. Sticking a rod into a spinning bicycle wheel stops the wheel movement as the rod hits against the bicycle frame. If a person is on the bicycle, he or she will fly over the handlebars and can be seriously hurt. The rod, after striking the frame of the bicycle, may fly right back out and hit you or someone else, potentially causing serious physical damage. Stopping others from energetically spinning can be just as dangerous to both them and yourself. Always approach this technique cautiously and with some trepidation. You are taking a serious energy risk with your spirit body if you choose to attempt it.

If you are considering intervening and stopping someone else from spinning, you need to be sure that you are moving your own energy well and your spirit body energy is flexible and nimble. You may need to jump out of the way from an energetic perspective when energy boomerangs back at you. Due to the strong energy release that can happen, make sure that there is geographical separation between the two of you to give the energy a chance to disperse somewhat before it reaches you. You will want to envision a shield that will block this incoming energetic shrapnel from hitting your spirit body.

To do this technique, you are going to act on the chakra that is causing the person's spirit body energy to spin out. Start by determining which chakra is causing the spinout. If you are sensitive to energy movement in the chakras, focus on the person's chakras to determine which one is causing the spin to occur. If you are not sure which chakra is causing the spinout, or you cannot sense chakra energy, you can use the words people are using when they are talking about how they are feeling to figure this out. Regardless, you should not try to stop the spinout energy unless you know which chakra is causing the issue. It is better to do nothing than to negatively affect a chakra that is moving energy properly or has been limiting the spinning energy from completely taking over the other's spirit body. A word of warning, if you negatively affect a chakra that is attempting to balance the energy rather than the chakra causing the problem it can cause a bigger energetic spinout.

When you are ready and know which chakra you need to act on, find a quiet place to focus and gather your energy. Remember, you do not even want to be in the same location as people you want to help with this energy technique. When you feel the energy is strong within you and you can focus your energy like a laser, envision the person with the spinning energy. Using your third eye, visualize the person until you can clearly see him or her. Place a temporary bubble or cocoon shield around them. Essentially, you are putting a "containment shield" around them to stop them from bleeding energy and to block energy from boomeranging back onto you or those who are around them. To avoid karmic backlash, you need to be certain that you do not add to their energetic crisis. Once the containment shield is in place, try to sense the direction they are spinning. Now focus on creating a white light energy spear that you are going to throw at their spirit body. This energy spear has branches that will catch hold of any chakras above and below the spinning chakra as well as the edges of their spirit body. The energy spear resembles a trident with claws at the tips instead of sharp points.

Focus your energy and throw your white light energy spear at the chakra causing the energy crisis within them. You should try this only once in a sitting. If you miss or the spinning does not stop, the universe is telling you that you cannot intervene to help them. That is okay. In this situation, the spinning might be a karmic payback for something they did. If the universe allows you to stop their spinning energy, then watch out for flying energy coming at you. After finishing this technique, you may have a dull headache or feel nauseous. Some of you will be physically sick after you stop another's energy spin due to energy motion sickness. This should pass fairly quickly after you meditate and ground your energy. Remember to thank the universe after you finish this technique for its help and allowing you to help your friend or loved one.

You might be wondering how recipients of this energetic intervention will feel after someone stops the spin. When it works, they notice that all of a sudden the spinning energy has stopped. Some feel numb or a little disoriented due to the sudden change in energy movement. Most people who have this technique done on their spirit body have a dull headache for a few days afterward and feel a little "spacey," or somehow disconnected from the situation. This sensation is just short-lived and should pass.

Chapter 12

RETURNING ENERGY

Whenever we release energy into the universe, the divine immediately assesses it and sorts it based on the energy type. Essentially, the universe moves this energy into different "buckets" depending on whether it is a request to manifest something, good wishes, healing requests, negative energy aimed to hurt another, and a host of other categories. From here, it sorts the energy by urgency and frequency of requests from people, and different angels might get involved to help fulfill the requests. Angels are ready and willing to manifest your desires and assist you as needed as long as it does not impinge on the free will of others. However, they decide how they will answer your request. If you want to try to control how they help, you are really limiting them to the point they decide that they do not want to be involved. Like us, they have the universal right to practice their free will. Therefore, it is always a good idea to be open to receiving the help given in the way they choose to answer your request.

Unfortunately, negative energy that we send out into the cosmos can get in the way of angels manifesting our desires. Essentially, whenever anyone puts out significant negative energy into the universe, it may end up obscuring energetic requests for help. If the angels cannot find the request, it is less likely that they will answer it. Sadly, some of the energy we send to the universe has the intent of causing some form of significant energetic injury to another or against ourselves. This is the energy released in a moment of anger or from our dislike of another or ourselves. There are times when we get in the way of blessings in our lives because we believe that we are not worthy of receiving gifts from the universe. Remember, we all make mistakes. Sometimes the person we need to forgive is our self before we feel that we can accept gifts and blessings from the universe. Regardless of whether we release negativity to the universe against others or ourselves, we are subject to the return of our own energy with this ill intent. Sometimes, our ill wishes for others quickly manifest within their lives. When this happens, our energetic payback on what we originally sent multiplies.

KARMA

Whenever I speak about the return of your energy and the effects on your life from past deeds, I use the word *karma* as the means through which the divine achieves this. In essence, karma is the consequence of the universal decision on the intent and strength of the energy we previously sent out into our world and to the universe. It assesses our guilt or innocence in any interaction we have with others or on our world. As we send our energy into our world and to the universe, regardless of whether it is with good, neutral, or bad intent, there is an energetic repercussion for doing so. When we send good, then our reward is good things or events manifesting within our lives. If you continually send out positive energy to others, the good is magnified within your life. If the energy is not good, then it returns to us in some form that is negative for us or for those we love. Most of the time, when we think of karma, what comes to mind is the universal backlash for acting against others for our personal gain; to hurt others physically or psychologically; to damage others' reputation; or to harm them in any other way. Regardless of the type of energy we send out into the universe, eventually karma is used to intervene and restore the energetic balance. Although it can take a long time for karma to appear within your life for things you did, it's to your benefit. If you did things that were not as good, it gives you an opportunity to change and make restitution for your prior actions.

It is easy to confuse repatriating energy with karma. Repatriating energy is energy that immediately returns to you after it is released due to another deflecting it and sending it back to you. This energy passes through all of your shields as though they are not there since it is simply your own energy repatriating with your spirit body. It is like sending an e-mail through a service provider to an e-mail ID that does not exist. The intended recipient did not get it, and there is a record with your service provider that the e-mail was not delivered. In turn, they send you an automatic "did not deliver" message. When you send out energy, the universe is the service provider in the e-mail analogy. The universe knows that you sent energy at another. It even knows the intent and content of the energy sent and that the recipient rejected the energy and returned it to you for repatriation. Even though your energy repatriated, you have just opened yourself to potential karmic energy return for the original intent of your energy even though nothing happened to the recipient.

Conversely, when karma is in play, there is a delay between the time you released the energy and when it returns. The delay is due to the universe reviewing the incident, determining the intent of all parties, and assessing guilt or innocence. Whenever we send out energy either directly or through our words, the universe decides if it is going to add a multiplicative factor to your energy. Do you remember Newton's law that every action has an equal and opposite reaction? Energetically, this principle also applies to our words and actions. Depending on the strength of the energy sent—the anger, intent to hurt, and a variety of other factors—the universe assesses the potential it had to hurt the intended victim. If it was positive energy in the form of good wishes or blessings for another, it determines the intent of this energy when determining the outcome. It also assesses their guilt and innocence in the situation that caused the release of energy. If someone deliberately antagonized you or did things to upset or hurt you over a long time, so that you finally broke and retaliated by sending out massive levels of energy against him or her, the universe knows this. When the energy release was a return of good to another who did good things for you, it also knows this.

It considers all aspects of the acts and energy when determining what it will do with the energy. At times, the universe destroys the energy because in the final assessment of the situation, it deemed your energy response to be "fair" or somehow "justifiable." Other times, the universe destroys it because the exchange of positive energy between two people equally benefited the other. Unfortunately—or maybe I should say fortunately—the universe destroys a lot of the negative energy that it receives and returns it to the grid for recycling. The reason is that after the final assessment of anger-fueled interactions, the damage sustained by both parties is considered to be relatively equal from an energetic perspective. This does not mean what either of you had done was right. It just means that you were both equally in the wrong. By destroying the energy, the universe has removed the energy associated with the event from both of you and is giving both of you a second chance to do things differently in the future.

However, there are times that the balance of energy is off and there is a victim of the energy exchange resulting in someone being hurt or disadvantaged in some way. The victim may have even called out to the universe to step in and rebalance the energy. After assessing the situation, if the victim was disadvantaged, the universe rebalances energy in many different ways. To list them all would take many, many books to write, since the universe tailors the balancing of energy on an individual basis. These energetic imbalances are very common and the leading cause is when we release anger or frustration energy into the universe.

When we are angry with someone, we release negativity against him or her to the universe. If we talk to others using mean energy, we compound the negative energy released to the cosmos. Although we have probably hurt another's feelings or made him or her angry due to the energetic attack, those who are better at sending out negative intent against others or hurting them emotionally can create karmic imbalances more easily than others can. If we are angry with people who did nothing wrong against us, they are "innocent" from a universal perspective. I have found that the universe always enacts karma on behalf of the innocent. Whenever you attack innocents, you can generally expect to receive three times the energy back that you originally sent, especially if they did nothing in retaliation for your outburst of anger and corresponding negative energy. If they are kind to you after you wounded them, they can increase the karmic payback you receive, which is sometimes far more than three times your original intent. At a minimum, when we say negative, hurtful things against others, we should probably expect to have negative, hurtful things said about us.

This type of karmic return is the most visible to others. We probably all know someone who spewed negative energy at another only to have something happen that causes others to spew negative energy right back at them. Although the return of energy may take a long time to manifest, when it does, this energetic return is like a heat-seeking missile that targets the person who started the energetic attack. Depending on the situation, by saying negative things about another, it can have a more serious and multiplicative factor applied. If you are doing this from a power position, you might find yourself stripped of a prestigious role you loved; or if it is at home, you might find yourself alone and realizing that the one you really love most in this world wants absolutely nothing to do with you. However, the way in which karma manifests the return of your energy is sometimes very creative, and it is not easy to attribute it to a single act you did. The reason for that is that karma is returning energy from several different situations in a single energetic package.

Earlier in this book, I mentioned that the energy we send out to the universe gathers. Regardless of whether we predominately send positive or negative energy, this energy begins to swirl in the universe and follows us in our lives. Over time, this collective of energy gets heavy. In some respects, the gathering of this energy is similar to rain clouds. As rain clouds pick up moisture from the atmosphere, they can get very heavy, and eventually they release the water vapor in the form of precipitation. The energy that we release to the universe also gathers and begins to swirl in the cosmos. As the cloud of energy consolidates and becomes heavy, eventually karma releases some of the pent-up energy back into our lives. If it is good energy, you will probably receive "showers" of good things happening in your life or in the lives of those you love. If it is negative energy, the converse is true.

For most of us, this cloud of energy is a mix of good and bad energy that has accumulated. When the showers of returning energy come, you will receive a mix of good and bad things, all happening around the same time to you and to those you love. As this mixed energetic shower falls in your life, it can make you feel confused or wonder why everything feels chaotic. Whenever you are going through a period when volumes of returning negative energy enter your life, remember it will eventually end. Most of us have done things or said things that hurt others that we regret. When you do things you are later sorry for doing, or saying things that hurt another, ask the universe for forgiveness. You should also ask the person whom you hurt for forgiveness. The next step is to do what you can in the physical world to make things right with the person you negatively affected. When you do this, you can limit the amount of negative energy in the universe that will eventually return to you. However, the universe knows whether your regret and restitution for what you did in the physical realm were fair and honest. If you are simply saying the word *sorry* hoping to eradicate the negative energy you released to the universe, it generally does not work—especially if the only reason you are sorry is that you want the energy to pass but still keep the benefits gained when you originally hurt the other.

Karma always rules when it comes to returning energy that you modified through repentance. My advice is to always consider the possible ramifications of things that you do. Although it can take a while for negative energy to return, unless you do something to destroy this energy through restitution, it will come back. If it is the result of someone hurting, betraying, or cheating you, karma sometimes waits until you stop sending out negativity about the situation before restoring the energetic balance. Regardless of what the universe decides in respect to your actions or the actions of others, through karma the divine determines whether the punishment has been sufficient. Some of you will receive energy from the universe notifying you that karma is returning to you. If it is anticipatory energy, it might be that karma is returning good to you or the universe is rewarding you or answering your prayers.

Some of you reading my book do not believe in a divine entity called karma that is righting the wrongs of this world. Rather, you might think that some of the negative things that occur in your life are simply a return of the energy that you put out against others into the cosmos. You might even refer to the return of this energy using different words. Regardless of how you label this return of energy, it does not negate the fact that this energy can and does return in many different forms. Past acts against others will have an effect in your life or the life of your family, or the return may even be delayed and affect you in your next lifetime. Only the divine knows when or how this return of energy and repercussions from past acts against others will manifest in your life. It is important to remember that not all karmic interventions are bad. At times, amazing, wonderful things happen for you when karma decides that you deserve the return of the good energy that you sent out to others in the form of good wishes, blessings, and acts of kindness.

REPEATING LIFE LESSONS

Thankfully, the universe in its wisdom and generosity often gives us the opportunity to repeat a life lesson if we acted in a way that was not to the highest good of all, or we didn't learn what they had wanted us to learn from the experience. As we experience repeating life lessons, it is a strong message to us to look within ourselves to figure out what we should do differently to generate the most positive outcomes for ourselves without causing negative consequences in the lives of others. This can be quite a challenge. Other times, the lesson is simply to teach us how to manage our energy more effectively to overcome a situation and grow from the experience.

There is a lot to know about managing your energy, and do not be hard on yourself if you find yourself repeating a life lesson. I hope that you will be a much quicker study than I am. At times, the universe repeats my life lessons several times until I finally "get it." If the universe did not think I learned what it wanted me to learn, or I did not handle the situation in the "best way" energetically, it sent the lesson back to repeat itself. Most of the time, it was with different people, but there was an uncanny similarity to the earlier life experience or situation. When a lesson repeated, I inwardly groaned, moaning that I had to "do it again" … and I even questioned why. Upon reflection, I knew that the universe in its divine wisdom was trying to help me to become the best version of myself. My wish was that I would get it right the first time. It definitely would save me a lot of angst if I did. I find that the first time I lived through these tough lessons was more than enough for me. I really do not want to have to repeat them.

You too might have noticed that as you move through your life's journey, the same situation or series of events presents itself repeatedly. Sometimes there are small variations as to who is involved or how the problem begins. However, you will probably find that the same common theme runs through it or that you must deal with someone with a personality similar to that of a person from a prior situation. Unfortunately, with each repetition, it becomes more difficult and challenging to work through. Why is this? The simple answer is that if it did not add something to it, it would essentially be "giving away the answer," which would defeat our soul's life purpose. We are to learn and grow from our experiences rather than the universe telling us what we should be learning or doing. When we internalize a lesson is when soul growth occurs. We need to "own" the learning process and try to determine what our soul can learn from this experience. Remember, the universe only does this if they feel that a do-over is needed for you to learn something or reinforce learning in some way. Thankfully, the universe does not make you live the same day over again until you get it "right." As a world, we probably would be still stuck in the dark ages today if it were to do that.

Common life lessons people experience relate to relationships or people you are in close proximity with on a near daily basis. It may even be associated with working with others. For example, you might find yourself subject to the leadership of a micromanager when you work best with a hands-off leader who empowers you to be your best. In this situation, working for a person who tries to control your every movement can feel like a soul-crucifying experience. If this is you, maybe the lesson you need to learn is how to return energy back to the sender. The lesson may be to learn how to protect your spirit body from people who try to control you in other ways. It may simply be that you need to release a little of the control you try to hold over your life and trust another to lead the way. Conversely, you may thrive under a micromanager who tells you exactly what he or she expects from you, but your current leader is completely hands-off and the lack of leader direction makes it difficult for you to know what is expected of you. This may be a lesson to teach you to take control of your life by reminding you that you need to live your own life, not the life another wants you to live. Although it can be tough to take charge of your life when you are used to others doing it for you, it can feel very empowering once you get started. The first step can be the scariest.

Remember, even though the situation you are in is difficult for you, another person may thrive in the same environment. The differences come from whether or not the situation affects an area that your soul needs to develop. If your soul is already an expert in navigating a situation, it is easy for your human trinity. When it is not, it is difficult. Unfortunately, sometimes your entire human trinity hurts when your soul is growing. An important thing to remember is that you can choose how your spirit responds to a situation. You are probably wondering why you just cannot skip a lesson that repeats that you find painful. It has been my experience that if the universe wants you to learn a lesson, it will keep presenting the situation, albeit in different ways, until your soul learns what it needs to learn. It doesn't allow you to skip the lesson.

Our souls learn so many things from our repeating life lessons. The goal of the lesson might be to teach us how to use grounding or shielding techniques to protect our energy body from negativity. Whenever you are in a situation dealing with negativity of others, it is a good time to practice your shielding techniques. Other times, the intent of the lesson is to teach you to stand up and move past the victim mentality in a way that is courteous and professional while taking back your personal power. The ability to regroup, stand up, and refuse to be the victim reminds your soul that it has the strength to overcome adversity and that you are worthy of having good things happen in your life. In difficult situations, the universe gives you the opportunity to practice controlling your energy and to learn techniques to stop the energetic spinning within you. Although this sounds easy, it can be a very difficult thing to implement if you feel like your life is spinning out of control.

At times, the lesson is far simpler than what is happening in your spirit body or soul. When your work life becomes hard, it may simply be a result of the universe telling you that you are holding a job in too high a position in your life. It might be trying to remind you that it is just a job, not who you are. Defining yourself should come from within your soul or as a joint decision of your human trinity and not as a result of how others perceive you or the "worth" attributable to you based on a job you do. If work consumes your thoughts to the degree that you are spinning even when you are not at work, then you probably should consider changing jobs. It may be the universe putting you in such an uncomfortable position at work because it wants to do something different. On the other hand, maybe the lesson is not to dedicate so much of yourself to a job. Instead, it is to teach you to turn your attention to committing more time and dedication to personal relationships unrelated to work. When you look within yourself, you may find the answer to this puzzle. In the meantime, I would recommend that you meditate to ground your energy. As long as you are spinning energetically, it is very difficult to hear what your soul is saying. In this state, you are more likely to make a decision based solely on what your physical body indicates you should do, which might not be in the best interest of your human trinity.

I must admit, I am a big fan of asking the universe to tell me exactly what I need to learn as I go through life situations, especially repeating life lessons. I have lost count of the times that I've told the universe that a nice, high-level overview of what it wants me to learn would be lovely. Unfortunately, it usually does not tell me. Rather, it lets me work through it, sometimes using trial and error, until I eventually get it "right" or as close to "right" as I can. When a situation stops repeating, I know I finally succeeded in learning the intended lesson. I must admit, there are times that the universe repeats the lesson many times before I get it right. During these times, I've realized that regardless of what the repeating lesson was, it was important to avoid letting myself be stuck in the angst of it. I also found that when a life lesson repeated, it progressively became worse and more challenging. Consequently, it was in my best interest to try to figure out the lesson and learn from it as quickly as I could.

I learned that the first step to handling a repeating life lesson is to pause and reflect on the situation. Then I walk through an internal checklist of things to consider as I try to figure out what it is I am to learn. Most repeating life lessons are associated with interpersonal relationships with others. Below is a list of some of the questions I consider when faced with a repeating life lesson and part of the struggle is associated with interacting with others.

What to ask yourself if a lesson repeats

1) What is the problem?
2) What are their personality characteristics? How do they differ from yours?
3) What energy body type are they?
4) What specifically are they doing to cause you emotional or mental pain?
5) How is this situation similar to what has happened to you in the past?
6) What is different about this situation this time?
7) What have others done to you that have happened before?
8) How did you react then?
9) How are you reacting now?
10) What did you do differently in the past?
11) What worked … and what did not?
12) Do you think that some things you tried in the past will work this time? Why or why not?
13) What lesson could you learn from the situation that you have missed in the past?
14) What can you do differently this time? This one is tough. This is where it might be a good idea to talk it over with an objective friend, or find someone who is an emotive intuitive to help you see through the chaos to reveal the different paths available to you. Unfortunately, lessons usually are to help you grow. If you like to avoid conflict and give in to others for the sake of

peace, it might mean you need to stand firm in your convictions regardless of whether it makes another angry. It may mean that you need to stand up to a bully. If this is the case, it can be terrifying.

15) How can you approach the situation with light and love? This one is sometimes simply asking the universe for guidance or help not to "throw" energy at them. That being said, if they are throwing energy at you, if you decide to simply "return it to the sender," the universe is fine with that. Just avoid adding a "boost" of your own energy with their repatriating energy.

Remember, actions are energy. How you react positively or negatively contributes to the outcome in all situations. By taking time to figure out what the lesson is and what you can learn from it gives you the insight needed to react differently and potentially avoid repeating the life experience. Sometimes from the most hurtful situations in your life, your soul grows the most. There are times when the life lesson is for the person who is hurting you and you are his or her last chance to get it right. If the lesson is for them, the beautiful thing is that once you have finished the lesson with them it doesn't repeat. If the lesson is for you, once you learned what the universe intends, it stops repeating. However, this invariably means that a new life lesson will soon present itself. When you are experiencing repeating life lessons, or any negative life experience where you feel as though your stability or sense of safety, happiness, or contentment eludes you, there are things you can do to help your spirit body feel better. The first step is to ground your energy. If you are sparking off or wasting your energy on non-necessary things, it affects your effectiveness in energetically responding to the situation in the most positive way possible.

It can be very worrisome for you as you are living through a difficult period in your life. You may feel that you are constantly in the middle of an energetic battle. Whenever you are living through any life lesson that you find difficult, consider reaching out to the universe for help. You may want to ask it for guidance and insight on how to act or speak, and you might even want to ask the universe how it will turn out. To do this, send a ping of energy to the universe with a question or request for help. Sometimes, the response is a sense of calm or peace to let you know that things are going to be fine. Other times it sends someone to you who offers advice that you immediately "know" is the right approach to take. Whenever you feel this way, ask the universe to help you by sending you energy to stay strong and reinforce your shields. Also, consider asking for the universe to send you peace and a knowing that everything is going to be just fine.

Next, reach out and pull in strength energy from those in your human relationship matrix. Let them know what is happening and what you need from them to help stabilize you. This can be tough when those to whom you directly connect are also going through a difficult time. But the beauty of the human relationship matrix is that when you help them stabilize and they are helping you, even though your lives are going through a tough time, you can help each other and divert some of your focus on what is causing your energy to spin. As you hold onto each other, the energy coursing through the cord connections can spread to secondary and tertiary connections can hold you firm. Although your primary connections feel like they are the fabric of a trampoline and someone is jumping on them, the secondary and tertiary connections become the springs and metal frame keeping you from falling apart. It is a great blessing we receive from our human relationship matrix. The ability to share energy and support each other gives us resilience that we cannot achieve if we looked only inside ourselves for strength or support. Whenever you find yourself in a repeating life lesson, or any difficult life lesson, remind yourself that it will eventually end. How fast sometimes depends on you.

Chapter 13

PUTTING ENERGY KNOWLEDGE INTO PRACTICE

Learning how to move your energy, how your chakra energy affects your human trinity, and how to use your energy to benefit your life is a great start. However, it cannot change your life for the better until you do something with the information. It can feel overwhelming, leaving you wondering how to put what you have learned into practical application in your life. Some of you reading this book may feel that it is just too much to do all at once. I agree. However, without taking the first step and starting out small, you are limiting your ability to find peace within yourself or create moments of tranquility in your life. I have found that one of the most powerful ways to live a more content life is controlling how I use my energy and draw refreshed energy into my spirit body.

The biggest question to ask yourself is whether you are ready to do the work. If you feel as though everything is working great for you and there is nothing further to do to manage your energy, you are very lucky. Unfortunately, many of us need to work at this to gain control over our energy and the energy received from others in order to achieve peace within ourselves. If we do not, there are significant energy effects within our spirit body. Many of us have allowed the negative energy around us to strike us and injure our spirit bodies. We might even have fallen into the trap of mismanaging our energy or having connections with others that have caused harm to our spirit bodies at some time in our lives. To heal and promote the movement of healthy energy within us, we have some work to do. For us, it may just be that we need to practice managing our energy in order to get good at it and do it automatically without having to think about it.

Learning how to control your energy puts you back in control of how your energy responds to your life experiences. If you are not sure where to start, a good first step is to assess your energetic abilities. How does your spirit body feel right at this moment? Can you feel energy churning within you? Is a chakra buzzing with energy but the energy is not going anywhere? What kind of people or experiences are you drawing into your life? Sometimes, a good way to figure out how you are resonating is to look at the people around you. Are they generally positive people, or are they negative? If you feel that they are negative, there is a chance that you too are resonating negative energy. Remember, we all have the ability to resonate negatively from time to time. The difference is that a negative person always resonates negatively and views everything, even good things, through a negative lens. The next question becomes, "Are you resonating in a manner that is to your highest good?" How effective are you in calming the churning energy within your spirit body? Remember, we all have energy churning within us at times. This really is a normal aspect of our human existence. If you are currently feeling your energy swirling within you, it can be the perfect time for you to start harnessing the energy and moving it in more positive ways to better your life. When you can feel your energy moving, you are in tune with your spirit body, even if the events causing the chaotic energy are negative or causes you concern.

Your spirit body is similar to your physical body in many ways. Using your energy and moving it through your spirit body is similar to exercising your physical body. When you exercise your physical body, it releases endorphins that make it feel better. A similar mechanism is at work within your spirit body. Drawing in new energy promotes the release of energy residue and is invigorating for your spirit body. Energy is the fuel that keeps your spirit body moving, healthy, and happy by allowing it to shed residual energy that can hold you back in some way.

When your spirit body is happy, it sends messages to your physical body letting it know that you are feeling good or at peace. This process infuses your entire human trinity with happiness, joy, or simply contentment in your life. If your physical body is unhappy, it still improves how your feel overall and can become a stepping-stone leading you to peace in your life.

However, when you do not use your energy, it can have a disastrous effect within your spirit body. Consider your physical body for a moment. If you do not use a limb, over time the muscles atrophy and it begins to shrivel. Eventually, you lose the ability to use it effectively and it feels weak if you try using it. Your spirit body is the same. If you do not move energy through it regularly, it too will get weaker and start wasting away, withdrawing further into your human trinity. Essentially, if you do not use your energy, your spirit body morphs into the equivalent of an extremely old person who can barely move around and has become a shadow of what he or she once was. To bounce back from that state takes a tremendous amount of work, heartache, and patience. It would be similar to having to learn how to walk again in your physical state after a traumatic accident that temporarily took away your ability to walk.

As human trinities, we are continually bombarded with energy in many different forms. Every day, we walk through energetic meteor showers thrown off by people everywhere we go. Having all of this energy surrounding us is energetically similar to being in the middle of an uprising where people are firing weapons, mines are exploding, and planes are flying overhead dropping bombs, threatening our very existence. Depending on the energy type and if it strikes you, it can have profound impacts on your spirit body. It is critical that you block this energy from entering your spirit body to prevent you from picking up the residual energy baggage from others. When doing this, you also need to be very aware of the energy you are releasing to the cosmos.

Whenever you get angry or upset or release any strong emotion, you release a tsunami of energy that spews out to the universe and at others which may cover everything around you. Remember, whenever you release energy into the cosmos at a person or a situation, you are responsible for the ramifications of that energy. In the heat of anger, you might feel that your words or intent was justified. However, after cooling off, you may realize that you were a little over the top. As I mentioned in the prior chapter, if in your anger you go too far in sending negative energy at another, it can lead to karmic reprisal. However, worrying about that can magnify the negative energy return. Instead, let the worry go and consider what you can do to mitigate the energetic return. I find that the best approach is to ask for forgiveness, mean it, and make things "right" for the person or people you hurt. These actions tend to negate some, if not all, of the negative energy from spiraling back at you. The beautiful thing about energy is that you have the ability to pull back your energy and turn it to dust. Since it is your energy, if you call it back, it comes. However, if you waited too long to call your energy back, the energy might already be affecting the other person. In that case, you can ask the angels to turn the remainder of the energy you sent to dust. To pull your energy back, simply say that you are pulling the energy back that you sent out at XXXX when you were very angry with him or her. Ask the universe to turn it to dust and shield the intended recipient from the harm you initially intended.

It is critical that you draw refreshed energy into your spirit body on a regular basis from the universal energy grid. This allows you to release the old energy and residual energy that you picked up during the day. Drawing in and then releasing old energy allows your spirit body to breathe. When you are drawing in energy, be sure to send it through all your chakras and out the opposite end. It does not matter if you pull it in through your taproot or on your physical body's breath. Remember, when you pull it in through the universal energy grid, send it through all of the chakras, visualize the energy swirling gently through the chakras, creating gentle suction to draw out the energy residue from your spirit body and replace it with new, revitalized energy. If you draw in energy through your taproot, send it up through each chakra until it reaches your mouth. Then blow out the residual energy from your mouth on your expelled breath. As you breathe in, pull in the energy and send it up through the brow and crown chakras, before sending it down through the remaining chakras to your base chakra. Then push it out through your toes.

If you struggle to feel the energy move, imagine the energy is moving up through your spirit body like soda bubbles move to the top of a glass. As the bubbles travel up within you, they stir up the energy residue and carry it to the outlet where you are removing your residual energy. If you are drawing the energy in on your breath, visualize suction from your taproot that is drawing the energy down through the chakras in a downward spiral.

Drawing energy into your spirit body is only one way that energy enters it. You also receive energy from others through ethereal umbilical cord connections or as direct strikes against your spirit body. To manage your energy effectively, you need to control how much of this energy from others you allow into your spirit body. Although you cannot stop your energy from repatriating, you can stop the influx of negative energy from others from entering you and pulling you down. This is where it is important to shield your spirit body to block direct strikes of energy. Installing filters in your shared cords is helpful in limiting the volume and type of energy that can enter.

There are times when moving energy becomes difficult or your energy feels stuck. When this occurs, it can manifest in feelings of dissatisfaction in life or in an inability to draw good things into your life. Whenever you have energy that is blocked or stuck within your spirit body, you need to act in order to restore movement. To restore movement through a chakra or other energy center in your spirit body, you need to remove the energy that is causing the blockage. A great way to remove some of this energy is to place a Septarian stone over the general area where the energy is stuck. The Septarian stone is a natural grounding stone that absorbs some of the negative energy or energy residue that clogs a chakra. Once some movement is restored, it is important to meditate to consciously draw in energy, sending it through the chakra and up into the next chakra. Remember, using a Septarian stone to restore energy gives temporary relief at best. You still need to determine the root-cause that is leading your energy to be stuck in that area. If you do not, you will continue to experience energy blockages in this area; eventually, the blockage becomes so consolidated that using a Septarian stone is limited in its ability to help restore movement.

When you release energy to the universal energy grid, you will sense this release of energy in a variety of different ways. If people release energy on their spoken word and it is going to the universe for manifestation, some feel that an essence of "power" goes with their words. There is sometimes a different resonance to their words. It is as though the words have additional strength and you have a sense of knowing that what you said is true and will manifest. Within your spirit body, you may even feel a small pulse of energy leave as you speak or that you draw in additional energy that goes with your words. Some of you will see a wisp of white smoke leave with your breath as you speak that quickly disappears. It can even be an intuitive sense that what you said is going to manifest. As long as you are not trying to manifest negative occurrences in the life of others, then this is fine. You have essentially let the universe know that you need this wish to manifest quickly and you are quite tired of waiting. It also sends a strong message that you have complete faith in the universe to manifest your desires.

When you are manifesting something, it is important that you clarify what you really want. Many of us are guilty of asking for the same thing over again if it does not manifest on a timetable that we might not have shared with the universe. The universe can be quite literal when it is manifesting what you ask for or when it is otherwise helping you. Try to be careful what you ask for, because it may manifest exactly as you asked—which might not be what you really wanted. It is also important that when you ask for something, you need to leave it with the universe to manifest instead of constantly taking it back and changing it, modifying it, or even re-requesting it. If you continually ask for the same general thing, but you keep changing the criteria of what you want, it changes the energetic resonance of what you asked for before. This new request is added to the prior request. Since the energy resonates differently from the last request, your request is put on the "waiting to fulfill" list until you can clarify what you want and stick with it. In essence, we send in our request to manifest something to the universe, but we keep pulling it back. When we do that, it takes a lot longer for the universe to manifest it.

My favorite illustration that I use to explain this concept is the analogy of what happens when we order food at a restaurant. When waiters or servers take your order, they take it to the kitchen to have your food made. However, if every few minutes, you call your server back to your table and keep modifying your order, the server takes it back to the cook. It does not take long before the cook decides to wait for you to make up your mind on what you really want. The cook does not want to start cooking your food only to have to start over. If you keep changing your order, the cook loses track of it, is confused as to which order is the most recent, or worse, is frustrated with you and does not want to cook anything for you.

The same applies to the universe. If you keep putting in a request only to pull it back to change it multiple times, the universe will essentially step back, figuratively cross its arms, and wait for you to make up your mind. It sometimes takes the universe a while to determine that you have stopped changing your requests before it starts the process to manifest your request—after it determines which one is the most recent. This often correlates to the time when you start thinking that the universe is not answering your prayers. It is difficult to fill your order if the universe is not sure what you really want. Instead, the universe waits for you to clarify what you want, settle on it, and give it a chance to manifest it before you change your mind again.

If what you are asking for is to the detriment of another—whether it is money, prestige, or any tangible item— the universe might grant what you are asking for. However, the manifestation of your wish might cause a long-term problem for your soul. Asking the universe to manifest something that isn't in your soul's best interest, or take from another may result in "selling your soul" for a short-term gain in this lifetime. Once your physical body dies, whatever physical thing you received stays on Earth and your prestige wanes as the years pass. Short-term, you have won. Long-term, your soul will be punished for what it did. It might mean that you come back in your next lifetime to an existence full of struggle in some form. Conversely, it may mean that someone you love will suffer through karma for your actions. How karma rights the wrong can take shape in many different ways, depending on the circumstances.

Unfortunately, there are times when the universe does not fulfill your request because you are asking for something that will interfere with your soul's life journey. By not giving you what you asked for, the universe in its divine wisdom is being kind, even though it may not feel that way. You might feel frustrated or angry that the universe is not manifesting what you believe you want or need. If the universe has not manifested something you asked for, reflect on what you asked for and consider the reasons why it did not manifest immediately.

When something you do is on the path of your manifesting something, you might see an energy swirl around your hand as you move it. It looks like you have just waved your hand through the wisp of white smoke above a candle but nothing is burning near you. When some of you are on a manifestation spree, you may find that whenever you touch anything that you are shooting off blue sparks of static electricity. However, if you get static electricity shocks off everything you touch, it can also be a warning that you are not adequately grounding your human trinity. In essence, your spirit body is telling you that it is "shorting out" due to energy overload. When this happens, be sure to practice meditation to ground your energy. Grounding will not negatively affect your ability to manifest good things in your life. However, if you are shorting out energetically and you are trying to manifest something, you may manifest what you are asking for, but what you receive may bring along a sense of unsettledness or anxiety. Remember, if your life journey includes a period of time when you will struggle in a specific way, the universe will not manifest a resolution to this struggle until after the assigned time or the lesson is complete.

HELP FROM THE DIVINE

As human trinities with the spark of the divine, we have the ability to call out to the universe for help. If you are in any situation where you feel that your physical being is in jeopardy, it never hurts to ask the universe for help. It may surprise you and send in an angel or a good Samaritan to rescue you. Sometimes, these good Samaritans appear and once the danger is over, they seem to "vanish." I suspect that some of these vanishing helpers, who seem to have no name and can never be found, are really angels in disguise. Conversely, the universe may send you a burst of energy that gives your physical body superhuman strength, speed, agility, or whatever else you need to escape or protect yourself. Then again, it might move you physically out of the path of harm.

Many of you reading this book have a story of how the universe stepped in and helped you out of a dire situation. I believe that we all have the ability to call on the universe for help. We just need to ask, even if the answer ends up being no. Without asking, you will never know with any certainty whether the universe will step in to help you out of what seems to be an impossible situation. If you ask for help but doubt that it will help you, then it probably won't. In the moment of doubt, you have essentially retracted your message asking for help. The fact is, unless you ask for help, you will never know if this is the time that it will.

When asking for divine help in a non-crisis situation where imminent physical danger is not present, we sometimes receive help from surprising entities. Some believe that if angels help, what you did was acceptable to the universe. Unfortunately, the entity helping you may not be "good," or it may be helping you with an expectation that you will do, or give up, something in return. Remember, there are good angels and those that are not. When asking for angelic help, you might actually receive help from a fallen angel or a watcher that is helping but masking itself and posing as a good angel. As shape shifters, they can make themselves look or act like anyone they choose. Regardless of who helps you, if it is against your soul's growth or if the request harms another, you are still responsible for the outcomes—how it affects others and the energetic intent. Any ramification of the act is your sole responsibility, and any associated karma will manifest in your life or in the lives of those you love. Whenever you ask for help, test the spirits who step forward to ensure that they are good and consider what you are asking them to do. If there is a potential for karmic backlash, you may want to reconsider what you are asking for.

Remember, the angels do not always give help whenever humans ask them for it. They get to practice free will, just like you. You can call upon them, but before they answer, they assess the situation and consult with the universe and karma to determine whether they agree to intercede on your behalf. Although good things happen to everyone regardless of whether you resonate pure "white" energy or a varying shade of gray, whether or not they help in moments of crisis is more complex than simply whether you are "good" or not. Sometimes, it is simply the unwavering faith that you put out to the universe that manifested what you asked for. It is important for everyone to realize that the universe blesses everyone with gifts regardless of how "good" he or she seems to be.

BE YOUR AUTHENTIC SELF

Whenever you want to promote healing within your spirit body, one of the most important gifts you can give yourself is to be your authentic self. If you spend your entire life trying to live up or down to the expectations of others, you have in essence allowed them to chain your spirit, and you have become who they wanted you to be, which may not necessarily be who your soul wanted you to grow into. In life, you are going to meet people that you want to accept you as a friend. However, if their resonance is different from yours, there will always be something off, causing a dissonance of energy between the two of you. Even if you pretend to be something you are not when you are with them to gain their acceptance, this sense of unsettledness or feeling as though you do not "fit in" can continue. When you live your life to please everyone else, it can be equivalent to prostituting your soul in your attempt to gain the acceptance of others especially if you act out their wishes by doing unkind things to others. Unfortunately, when we harm others, we are subjecting our own human trinity to karmic reprisal. It is your free will to choose to live this way. However, this way of living can obstruct your spirit from growing and result in your spirit body contracting within your physical body until you are a shadow of who you could have been.

If you choose to be your authentic self, your soul grows. Remember, although our souls are from the divine, they are not perfect. Life lessons allows you to grow past issues where you did not act in your soul's best interest as you strived to become the person your soul wanted to become in this lifetime. As your soul grows, you may find that you lose your connections to some people in the process. This is not always a bad thing. Sometimes, people are in your lives for a time, and then they leave. Although it can be very sad to lose once-close connections, it is sometimes fate that they leave because they were never intended to be in your life forever. They may have been the catalyst to start you on your path for healing. While they were in your life, they were very important to you.

Being your authentic self means you do not need to justify where you are in your soul's development. Remember, some people have more they need to learn in this lifetime, while others do not have as much. Regardless of what your journey contains, everyone who crosses your path who plays a role in your life is someone who was important in your journey. They may have been people who held out their hand and asked you to trust them and energetically jump to a better place, leaving behind the hurt and painful energy residue that was eating your spirit body alive. Regardless of the people in your life, try not to define yourself based on the perceptions others have of you. How they define you to be might really be a projection of who they are. Accepting a negative view of yourself may cause you to discount the innate goodness within yourself. However, if those around you think you are virtually perfect and cannot imagine that you could do any wrong against another, they can also be an obstruction to your soul's growth. If you simply accept their assessment that you are "perfect," it stalls your soul in its progress to continue growing into the best version of yourself. By ceasing to strive, your soul ceases to grow.

Being your authentic self allows you to embrace who you are as an energy being, accepting that you are not perfect and acknowledging that there are things your soul needs to learn to promote growth. It's accepting that you are a human trinity who has the ability to enact change within your physical world by using the universal energy gifted to you and that you have a responsibility to use your energy wisely. Your spirit body has the ability to manifest happiness in your life if you only believe that you can do it. This does not mean that the hurtful words or actions of others will not bother you. It will. Just remember that by hurting you with their words or actions, they are limiting their own spirit's growth, and storing up karmic reprisal in their own lives, which is sad. There are times when you may wish that you selected a different spirit body type to use in this lifetime. Acknowledging the spirit body you have, and loving the gifts it gives you, will start you on your path to overcoming your weaknesses and building on your strengths.

Regardless of the situation you are in, when you are your authentic self, your words, thoughts, and deeds resonate with your spirit body. When you are true to who you are and the gifts you have, then you are less likely to get yourself into energetic trouble. Whenever you overestimate your ability, you can stretch the abilities of your spirit body beyond what it can do, which can result in your burning out chakras or giving up pieces of your own spirit body in your attempts to help others. Over time, this will leave you as a shell of what you can be. Remember, it is always best to underestimate your abilities. When you do this, it ensures that you do not accidentally go too far energetically and require someone with strong energy skills to bail you out.

CONNECTING TO YOUR HIGHER SELF

Although you hear of the importance of connecting with your higher self, it is important to realize that you can always do it. Your higher self is your soul, which is the essence of your authentic self, and is the divine spark of energy driven through your human trinity by your sona. Without this connection, you would not be alive. However, even though you are connected, you may not always hear what your soul is trying to tell you due to loudness of a "voice" in your head that drowns out the messages from your soul. At times, this voice is the residual energy left behind from a hypercritical voice in your head from someone who continually told you how you were "wrong," "mistaken," or even "bad." Sometimes this voice goes on about what has gone wrong in your life, how you made bad decisions, why you are not "good enough," or other negative messages. At times, this is your own voice talking badly about yourself. This hypercritical voice comes from the residual energy left behind when others criticized you, fairly or not, that is stuck in your spirit body or comes from your physical body. Typically, your soul is trying to push you forward rather than tearing down your human trinity. When this voice is loud, it is very hard to hear the small voice of your soul telling you that you have the spark of the divine in you and not to be so critical of yourself. Trying to hear your soul's voice can be like trying to hear someone who is whispering to you at a concert where it is loud with music, screaming fans, and the noise of a crowd who are living in the moment. This can be very difficult.

To promote the connection to the messages of your higher self, you need to move into a brain state where alpha waves take over. When your brain is using alpha waves, it ceases to have conscious thoughts or to think of specific things. It is at this time when your spirit body opens its energetic wings to connect to the divine source of life. While connected to the divine, your spirit body has the ability to connect to the Akashic records to receive moments of divine inspiration or a knowingness of what you need to do to improve your life. You may be wondering how to do this. To be able to hear your soul, you need to find a way to quiet the noises in your head, spirit body, and physical environment. The first step is to find somewhere where you can just "be," where you are safe, at peace, and feel soothed. For some, this is sitting outside with only the sounds of nature around them. Others find sanctuary inside their home in a quiet place. Once you have an environment where it is quiet and peaceful around you, get comfortable. Whether you sit, stand, or lie down is up to you. The key is to feel physically comfortable. Now you are ready to turn your attention inward.

Start by assessing the energy flow within you. Is it feeling calm, chaotic, swirling, etc.? If you are not feeling calm, you will need to calm your energy before you try to reach your higher self. When your physical body and internal brain dialogue are loud, it can be so noisy that it is enough to drown out everything else. I like to start this process using meditation. Once I have calmed my breath and have turned my awareness inwards, I focus on the energy movement in my spirit body. In the beginning, I found it helpful to keep a journal of how my energy was moving in my spirit body to get a better idea of what my "resting" energy state felt like. I found that when I was going through a very stressful life phase, even though I thought I had achieved my energetic resting state, when I later reflected on how my energy felt compared to my journal, I realized that although I had successfully calmed my energy, I still had some work to do.

In my resting state, I focus on pulling down energy from the universe to replenish my human trinity. As my spirit body calms, I reach my energy up to the divine to become one with the universe. Focusing energy inward gave me the opportunity and the time to figure out how I primarily draw energy from the grid. Then I look back on myself from an objective perspective. I listen carefully to what my soul has to say. When it speaks, it is the quiet voice within you guiding you or reassuring you that everything will work out fine. In this state, I consider how I acted during the day and examine whether I always acted to the highest good of everyone, or in my own self-interest. Listening to my soul, I get an objective view of how I did, which does not always match up to how I thought I did. I consider what I have done well, and the moments in my day when I could have handled a situation or reacted in a more positive way.

The messages from your soul tend to be blunt and are not always things that you want to hear. As you listen, you will probably find that your soul has suggestions on how you could have handled moments in your day in a way that would have worked out better for everyone. When you are receiving any difficult messages from your soul, try to remind yourself that the first step of growth is realizing that you have an area requiring some additional development. In our human trinity form, we are perfection in our imperfection. We will make mistakes. It is expected. However, by listening to our soul, the divine essence of ourselves, and following its advice that is in our highest good, we become our authentic self. This view of you is judgment free and may be a different person from how you present yourself in life. It can also help you avoid the pitfalls that negatively affected your soul's path in prior lifetimes. Taking the time to become the best version of yourself can cause a tremendous spiritual awakening.

Unfortunately, we sometimes let life push us into corners where we come out fighting and reveal the worst version of ourselves. A view of ourselves that we may not even like. Through meditation, you have the ability to rediscover your authentic self as well as your core beliefs. When you take the time to see yourself through an objective lens, you can discover who you really are and what drives you forward. It promotes awareness of "why" you reacted as you did, giving your brain a chance to figure out how it can react differently the next time. Through this self-awareness, you might realize that you have been overly critical of yourself. Within each of us is the divine. Whether you listen to your soul's voice, reflect on your actions, or manage your energy, the decision is up to you. During your physical life here on Earth, your spirit body writes on your soul about your success in managing your energy in this lifetime, the decisions you made, and your impact on others. Try to make the words written as positive as possible, and something you can personally feel proud of accomplishing.

Afterword

You are pure energy encapsulated within a physical body. Through our human trinity, the universe gave us the amazing gift of multiple consciousnesses. It also gives us the ability to fully integrate and act as one being while retaining the ability for aspects of our being to act alone. As human trinities, we have access to the divine and life-sustaining energy from the universal energy grid. We also have the ability to live out our free will within our human form. As a divine spark of energy, we have the ability to send and receive energy in many forms through our spirit body. Our ability to connect to others, the world, and the divine is a wonderful gift that we can use to make this life experience the most positive one so far. Drawing on strength from our human relationship matrix, we can join our energy, support others, and overcome difficult life phases. Whether or not we choose to draw on the energy from our matrix or from the universal energy grid is a reflection of how we choose to enact our free will in our lives.

By becoming one with your spirit, you have the divine ability to become your authentic self, who can grow into the person your soul aspires to become. Although we all will make mistakes using our energy, we have the ability to take back our energy and rectify situations in both the physical and energetic planes. Using your energy and drawing on energy from the divine, you have the ability to manifest good things in your life. Regardless of how you choose to use your energy, it is your choice. My hope for you is that the information I shared in this book helps you understand who you are from an energy perspective, the beauty of your human trinity, and the powerful connection you have with the divine. I also hope it teaches you why you are truly an amazing being within the cosmos, and have the ability to manage your energy and find peace in your spirit.

Glossary

Term	Definition
Ancient knowledge	This is knowledge and information given to the ancients from the angels.
Aura	The manifestation of your spirit body's energy as energy resonances that some perceive as colors.
Chakras	Energy centers within the spirit body.
Energy body	It is your spirit body, aura, and shields.
Energy cramps	This is the physical manifestation of moving massive amounts of energy or having powerful swirling energy within your spirit body in the area of your physical body's bowels.
Energy dust/particles/residue	Residual energy left behind by energy beings and their interactions with others and the world.
Energetic earthquake	Any experience that is life-changing, shakes your human trinity, and causes your sona to drive energy in the opposite direction of what your energy being prefers.

Term	Definition
Energy chatter	This is the energy 'noise', vibrations and messages sent through shared cords using SOS communications that are not urgent. These messages share how the sender feels as they send a moment by moment energetic update on their day.
Energy high	Occurs when you are receiving energy from a new connection that distorts your energy, leading to feelings of wonder, newness, or empowerment.
Energy motion sickness	This is the physical manifestation of moving massive amounts of energy or having powerful swirling energy within your spirit body in the area of your physical body's stomach and/or small intestine.
Energy shower	Your returning energy that you sent to the cosmos after karma has decided to release it.
Energy transfer	This is when someone knowingly sends a packet of energy to another as a care package. It may also be the result of an unconscious movement of energy from one person to another.
Energetic umbilical cords	Ethereal energy connections between the people we love or care about and ourselves, used to share energy, love, and support.
Filters	An energetic barrier installed in shared umbilical cord connections to block any negative or residual energy from entering your spirit body.
Fire whirl	Occurs when fire energy people draw in energy quickly from their environment and cord connections, mixing it with their fire energy to create a tornado of fire energy.

Term	Definition
Human trinity	This is the triad of humanity resulting from the connection of your physical body, spirit body, and soul through the sona.
Human relationship matrix	A group of connections joining us to others through which we give and receive energy; it is our energetic safety net to help us retain our connection to the divine.
Infinity loop sona	An infinity loop sona is an oblong-shaped energy belt, shaped like a figure eight, connecting our soul, spirit body, and physical body.
Karma	This divine entity determines guilt and innocence and doles out justice to all spirit bodies.
Love fog	The energetic state where one is infused with energy from a new love, feel euphoric, protected, strong, distracted, or invincible and are not monitoring how this relationship is affecting their human trinity or cord connections to others.
Multiple consciousness	This is the result of the receipt of information from your soul, spirit body, and physical body. The information provides a different perspective of how to approach a situation or problem.
Residual energy dust	Energetic waste left behind within your spirit body after interactions with others and the world.
Residual energy	Energy left behind after a human interaction or experiencing a life situation where emotions or spirit body energy is released.
Shields	An energetic barrier used to deflect incoming unwanted energy from others.

Term	Definition
Simple loop sona	A simple loop sona is an oblong-shaped energy belt that connects our soul, spirit body, and physical body.
Sona	This divine connection forms the human trinity between our spirit body, physical body, and soul.
SOS transmission	A series of short, strong bursts of energy through a cord that requests some type of action of the recipient. These can be *focused* or *general* transmissions depending upon the audience to which it is sent.
Spirit	Your soul and spirit body working together through your life experiences.
Spirit body	Your spirit body is what animates your human form, and connects to the energy grid, others, and the world around you. Through it, you act out the essence of who you are as dictated by your soul.
Taproot	This is the means by which all spirit bodies connect to the universal energy grid.
Two-way communication network	How your physical body and spirit body communicate through your brain stem and into the central nervous system, causing you human trinity to act as a single being.
Undertow energy	A phenomenon that affects those with water spirit energies when churning energy within their spirit body creates a downward draw in their energy. This state causes a general sense of feeling down or energetically held back
Universal energy grid	This is the universal source of divine energy sustaining all life.

Taking Back Your Joy of Living

An Introduction to Managing Your Personal Energy

This book will teach you how to manage your energy and reclaim your power over how you energetically experience life. Every day, you are the recipient of energy from your world, the people in it, and as a result of your life experiences. Sometimes, energetic blows to your spirit can have lasting effects that become barriers to feeling joyful in your life. However, it doesn't need to stay that way. This book explores a variety of ways to shield your spirit from energy attacks, as well as how to block negative energy from entering your spirit body though the connections you share with others. By managing this energy, it allows you to be present in the lives of those you love without taking on the angst of their life struggles within your spirit in addition to your own.

Although you can't change events decreed by fate, you can choose to change how your spirit energetically reacts to what happens to you. Using the skills and techniques explained in this book allows you deflect negative energy, draw in positive energy and enrich your life. This will start you on your path to *Taking Back Your Joy of Living*.

Notes

Notes

Notes

Notes

Notes

Notes

Notes

Notes

Printed in the United States
By Bookmasters